*P*resented to:

_____

*P*resented by:

_____

*D*ate:

_____

GOD'S LITTLE
DEVOTIONAL BOOK

Special Gift Edition

Honor Books
Tulsa, Oklahoma

2nd Printing

God's Little Devotional Book, Special Gift Edition
ISBN 1-56292-528-8
Copyright ©1998 by Honor Books
P.O. Box 55388
Tulsa, Oklahoma 74155

Devotions drawn from *God's Little Devotional Book;* manuscript prepared by W. B. Freeman Concepts, Inc., Tulsa, Oklahoma.

Introduction

IN this newly enhanced version of the best-selling *God's Little Devotional Book*, you'll not only feed your mind on inspirational anecdotes, but you'll feast your eyes on equally inspiring artwork.

If you're looking for the perfect gift, this gorgeous book is fit to grace even the most discriminating person's coffee table. If you're the recipient of this thought-provoking book, you'll find it motivating, challenging, and encouraging. These stories will inspire you with doses of wit and wisdom.

This is not just another pretty book destined to gather dust on the shelf. You'll want to return to it again and again for enlightenment and renewed vision. All the devotions are tied to a scripture, providing the life-giving power in the Word of God to back up the principles contained in the quotes and stories.

God's Little Devotional Book, Special Gift Edition is intended to do just that—provide you a much-needed, often-missed devotional time with God. It can provide a stimulating addition to your morning coffee, a quick pick-me-up on your lunch hour, or a relaxing wind-down at the end of the day. Whenever and wherever you choose to read it, you will be refreshed, energized, and prepared to face another day.

The grass may look greener on the other side, but it still has to be mowed.

ONE day, a stonecutter delivered a slab of stone to a merchant. Seeing all the merchant's wonderful goods, the stonecutter said, "I wish I was a merchant." In the twinkling of an eye, his wish was granted. Sometime later, the hot sun beat down upon the man and he said, "I wish I was the sun—greater than any man." Instantly, he became the sun. He was happy for a time, until a cloud came between him and the earth. He said, "That cloud overshadows me. I wish I was a cloud." Again, his wish was granted. He was content until he came to a mountain, which wouldn't let him pass. He said, "That mountain is greater than I, I wish I was a mountain." Forthwith, he became a mountain and he thought, *Now I am the greatest of all!*

But one day a little man carrying a hammer and chisel climbed up the mountain and began to tap away at it. The mountain, unable to stop him, said, "That little man is greater than I, I wish I was a stonecutter." Once again his wish was granted and the stonecutter remained happy and content ever after.

Be content with such things as ye have.

Hebrews 13:5

*P*atience is the ability to keep your motor idling when you feel like stripping your gears.

8

AN old train was puffing its way slowly through the countryside when suddenly, it lurched to a stop. The only passenger in the three-car train quickly rose to his feet and went to find the conductor. "Why have we stopped?" he demanded. "I'm a salesman and I have an appointment in less than an hour in the next town!"

The conductor smiled, "Nothing to worry about, sir. Just a cow on the tracks. Gotta wait her out." The salesman returned to his seat, fuming and fidgeting until the train began to creep forward again. It chugged along for a mile or two and then ground to a halt once again.

This time the conductor found the salesman. "Don't worry sir," he said. "We'll be on our way shortly." The exasperated salesman asked, "What now? Did we catch up to the cow again?"

What the salesman didn't know was that the train's schedule *allowed* for these temporary delays. He easily made it to his appointment, but he was worn to a frazzle by his frustration.

God's plan for our lives allows for temporary delays. We will enjoy life much more when we respond to these delays with patience, rather than frustration.

He that is slow to anger is better than the mighty;
and he that ruleth his spirit than he that taketh a city.
Proverbs 16:32

*R*emember the banana—when it left the bunch, it got skinned.

WHEN we see the familiar V-formation of a flock of geese flying north for the summer or south for the winter, we are reminded of the changing seasons. The often untold story of the geese, however, teaches us the value of teamwork.

What many don't know is that when one goose becomes sick or wounded, it never drops out of formation alone. Two other geese also fall out and follow the suffering goose. Once on the ground, the healthy birds protect and care for the frail goose, even throwing themselves between the weakened bird and possible predators. They stay with him until he is either able to fly, or is dead. Then, and only then, do they launch out. In most cases, they wait for another group of geese to fly overhead and join them, adding to their safety and flying efficiency.

If only we human beings would care for one another this well! God's design is for us to grow and thrive in our relationships. When we isolate ourselves and cut each other off, we become sickly and weak. However, when we help others and allow others to help us we are strengthened, and everyone is enriched.

Not forsaking the assembling of ourselves together,
as the manner of some is; but exhorting one another:
and so much the more, as ye see the day approaching.
Hebrews 10:25

*M*any a good man has failed
because he had his wishbone where his
backbone should have been.

THERE once was a young boy who ran with a neighborhood gang. In later years, he recalled that while he had wished for a better life, he didn't know that a gang was not the way to achieve it. An older friend finally came to him and made him realize how much he was hurting his hard-working mother, as well as how much he was limiting himself. He said, "He told me that it didn't take guts to follow the crowd, that courage and intelligence lay in being willing to be different."

The young man left the gang, put away self-pity, and began to do something with his life. He developed his physical potential and within a few short years, became a sensational athlete. Starring in football, basketball, baseball, and track at UCLA, he was the first person at the university to win awards in all four sports. He went on to play pro football with the Los Angeles Bulldogs before being drafted for World War II. After the war, he switched to baseball and signed with the Brooklyn Dodgers, which made Jackie Robinson the first black player in major league baseball.

Wishing doesn't get you there; doing does.

Be strong and of a good courage; be not afraid,
neither be thou dismayed: for the LORD thy
God is with thee whithersoever thou goest.
❧ Joshua 1:9 ❧

*I*f at first you don't succeed, try reading the instructions.

A YOUNG ensign had nearly completed his first overseas tour of duty when he was given an opportunity to display his ability at getting the ship underway. With a stream of crisp commands, he had the decks bustling and soon, the ship was steaming out of the channel.

The ensign's efficiency had been remarkable. In fact, the deck was abuzz with talk that he had set a new record for getting a destroyer underway. Glowing in his accomplishment, the ensign was not surprised when another seaman approached him with a message from the captain. He was, however, a bit puzzled to find that it was a radio message, and he was aghast when he read, "My personal congratulations upon completing your underway preparation exercise according to the book and with amazing speed. In your haste, however, you have overlooked one of the unwritten rules—make sure the captain is aboard before getting under way."

God's Manual for Life, the Bible, is our instruction manual for getting our lives underway. Still, we must never become so bound to the book that we forget its Author and the relationship He desires to have with us on our voyage.

Take fast hold of instruction; let her not go:
keep her; for she is thy life.
Proverbs 4:13

Decisions can take you out of God's will but never out of His reach.

IN *A Closer Walk*, Catherine Marshall tells about the struggle she experienced after writing a novel titled *Gloria*. After two-and-a-half years of work, the project was abandoned. To her, the shelved manuscript was "like a death in the family."

While attempting to reconcile her conflicting emotions, Marshall spent time at a retreat. There, she reread a Bible story about a time when poisonous snakes filled the Israelite camp. The people recognized the snakes as a punishment for their sin, and cried out in repentance. The Lord told Moses to "make a [bronze] snake and put it up on a pole; anyone who is bitten can look at it and live" (Numbers 21:8 NIV).

Marshall realized that just as the Israelites took that which had hurt them and lifted it up to God for healing, we can take our own mistakes and sins, lift them to God, and trust Him to heal us. She writes, "When any one of us has made a wrong turning in our lives through arrogance or lack of trust or impatience or fear—God will show us a way out." God always knows where we are and how to get us back on His path.

If we are faithless, he will remain faithful,
for he cannot disown himself.

2 Timothy 2:13 NIV

Patience is a quality you admire in the driver behind you and scorn in the one ahead.

ON a Friday evening, just as the light turned green, his car stalled. All his efforts to start it again, failed. A chorus of honking instantly arose from the cars behind him.

Feeling just as frustrated as everyone else eager to get home for the weekend, he finally got out of his car and walked back to the car behind him. He waited for the driver to roll down his window, then said, "I'm sorry, but I can't seem to get my car started. If you'll go up there and give it a try, I'll stay here and blow your horn for you."

A person who is chronically impatient rarely makes anyone else go faster or arrive earlier. Instead, the effects are usually negative—affecting the impatient person as well as others. Accidents occur more frequently when we are in great haste. Ulcers, headaches, and other health problems quickly develop. And relationships are more readily strained.

To battle your impatience, try giving yourself ten extra minutes every day. Get up ten minutes earlier in the morning. Leave ten minutes earlier for work, and so forth. You will arrive at the end of your day feeling much more clear-headed and relaxed.

Patience is better than pride. Do not be quickly provoked in your spirit, for anger resides in the lap of fools.
Ecclesiastes 7:8-9 NIV

There is a name for people who are not excited about their work—unemployed.

20

THOMAS Edison, who held 1,093 patents for his inventions—which included the electric light bulb, phonograph, and motion-picture camera—sold the rights to many of his inventions to Western Union and other large companies. As a result, over time, others made far more money from Edison's inventions than he did, but this didn't seem to bother him a great deal. He once said, "I don't care so much about making my fortune as I do for getting ahead of the other fellow." Edison's greatest desire was to be both the first and the best in his field, to out-invent everybody he could. He worked tirelessly but with joy.

Edison eventually established Menlo Park, the world's first factory built specifically for the production of inventions. It was a forerunner of the private research laboratories now maintained by many large companies. At Menlo Park, Edison promised to turn out "a minor invention every ten days and a big thing every six months or so." At one point, he was working on forty-seven new things at once.

Other inventors may have been richer than Edison, but virtually no inventor has ever been more successful. For him, enthusiasm and employment were inextricably bound together!

And whatsoever ye do, do it heartily,
as to the Lord, and not unto men.
Colossians 3:23

*T*oo many churchgoers are singing "Standing on the Promises" when all they are doing is sitting on the premises.

22

THE story is told of a little boy who went on a blueberry-picking hike with his mother and aunt. He brought along the smallest pail possible. While the others worked hard at picking berries, he lolled about, chasing a butterfly and playing hide and seek with a squirrel. Soon it was approaching time to leave. In a panic, he filled his pail with moss and then topped it off with a thin layer of berries. His mother and aunt commended him highly for his effort.

The next morning his mother baked pies, and she made a special "saucer-sized" pie just for him. He could hardly wait for it to cool. Blueberry pie was his favorite! He could see the plump berries oozing through a slit in the crust, and his mouth watered in anticipation. However, when he sunk his fork into the flaky crust, he found—under a thin layer of berries—moss!

Many people want to experience the fullness of God's promises in their lives, but they are unwilling to do the work that goes along with them. The majority of the promises found in the Bible are if-then statements—if we do our part, God will do His.

That ye be not slothful, but followers of them who through faith and patience inherit the promises.
❧ Hebrews 6:12 ❧

Some people complain because God put thorns on roses, while others praise Him for putting roses among thorns.

HERE'S the classic definition of the pessimist and the optimist: The pessimist will see a half-filled glass as being half empty, while the optimist will see it as half full. We could add to that description: The artist will see it as a vase, the pragmatist as a means of quenching thirst, the scientist as H_2O.

Consider the benefits of choosing the optimistic bent, as described in this poem:

> Two frogs fell into a deep cream bowl,
> One was an optimistic soul;
> But the other took the gloomy view,
> "I shall drown," he cried, "and so will you."
> So with a last despairing cry,
> He closed his eyes and said, "Good-bye."
> But the other frog, with a merry grin
> Said, "I can't get out, but I won't give in!
> I'll swim around till my strength is spent.
> For having tried, I'll die content."
> Bravely he swam until it would seem
> His struggles began to churn the cream.
> On the top of the butter at last he stopped
> And out of the bowl he happily hopped.
> What is the moral? It's easily found.
> If you can't get out—keep swimming around!

Finally, brethren, whatsoever things are true, whatsoever things are honest, whatsoever things are just, whatsoever things are pure, whatsoever things are lovely, whatsoever things are of good report; if there be any virtue, and if there be any praise, think on these things.

Philippians 4:8

*T*he bridge you burn now may be
the one you later have to cross.

WHEN Abraham Lincoln was campaigning for the presidency, one of his archenemies was Edwin McMasters Stanton. Stanton hated Lincoln, and often used the bitterest diatribes in an attempt to degrade him in the eyes of the public.

In the process of choosing a cabinet after his election, when it came to deciding who would fill the important office of Secretary of War, President Lincoln chose Stanton! The president's inner circle erupted in an uproar. Numerous advisors came to Lincoln saying, "Mr. President, you are making a mistake. Are you familiar with all the ugly things he has said about you? He is your enemy. He will sabotage your programs."

Lincoln replied, "Yes, I know Mr. Stanton. But I find he is the best man for the job."

As Secretary of War, Stanton gave invaluable service to his nation and his president. After Lincoln was assassinated, many laudable statements were made about Abraham Lincoln, but the words of Stanton remain among the most poignant. Standing near Lincoln's coffin, Stanton called Lincoln one of the greatest men who ever lived and said, "He now belongs to the ages."

When we treat an enemy with God's love, we earn their respect.

If it be possible, as much as lieth in you,
live peaceably with all men.
Romans 12:18

The measure of a man is not how great his faith is, but how great his love is.

IN 1873, a Belgian Catholic priest named Joseph Damien DeVeuster was sent to minister to lepers on the Hawaiian island of Molokai. He arrived on the island in high spirits, hoping to build a friendship with each of the lepers. He built a chapel, began worship services, and poured his heart out to the lepers, but all seemed futile. No one responded to his ministry.

Finally, after twelve years of struggling, Father Damien decided to leave. Wringing his hands as he stood on the dock waiting to board the ship, he looked down at his hands and noticed some mysterious white spots on them. Feeling some numbness, he knew immediately what was happening—he had contracted leprosy!

Father Damien returned to the leper colony and to his work. Word quickly spread and within hours, hundreds gathered outside his hut, fully identifying with his plight. And the following Sunday, when Father Damien arrived at the chapel it was full! He began to minister from the empathy of love rather than the distance of theology and ideas, and his ministry became enormously successful.

Those who receive your love today will be much more receptive to hearing about your faith tomorrow.

And now these three remain: faith, hope and love.
But the greatest of these is love.
1 Corinthians 13:13 NIV

$\mathcal{R}$eal friends are those who, when
you've made a fool of yourself,
don't feel you've done a permanent job.

ONE of the most noble friendships in literature is that of Melanie and Scarlett O'Hara in Margaret Mitchell's classic, *Gone with the Wind*. Melanie is characterized as a woman who, "always saw the best in everyone and remarked kindly upon it." Even when Scarlett tries to confess her shameful behavior toward Ashley, Melanie's husband, Melanie says, "Darling, I don't want any explanation. . . . Do you think I could remember you walking in a furrow behind that Yankee's horse almost barefooted and with your hands blistered—just so the baby and I could have something to eat—and then believe such dreadful things about you? I don't want to hear a word."

Melanie's refusal to believe ill of Scarlett leads her to passionately desire to "keep Melanie's high opinion. She did not care what the world thought of her or what Ashley or Rhett thought of her, but Melanie's estimation of her must persevere." As Melanie lays dying, Scarlett faces her deep need for Melanie's pure and generous friendship: "Panic clutching at her heart, she knew that Melanie had been her sword and her shield, her comfort and her strength." In two words, Melanie had been Scarlett's *true friend*.

Beareth all things, believeth all things, hopeth all things, endureth all things. Charity never faileth.

Be careful that your marriage doesn't become a duel instead of a duet.

MINISTER and newspaper columnist George Crane tells of a wife who came to his office full of hatred toward her husband. Fully intending to divorce him she said, "Before I divorce him, I want to hurt him as much as he has me."

Crane advised her to go home and act as if she really loved her husband. "Tell him how much he means to you," he said. "Praise him for every decent trait. Go out of your way to be as kind, considerate, and generous as possible. Spare no efforts to please him, to enjoy him. Make him believe you love him. Then, drop the bomb. That will really hurt him."

"Beautiful!" the woman exclaimed. She enthusiastically did as he had suggested, acting as if she loved him. Two months later she returned to Crane, who asked, "Are you ready now to go through with the divorce?"

"Divorce!" she said. "Never! I discovered I really do love him!"

Actions can change feelings. Lasting love is based on a decision, not just an emotion or feeling. Motion can result in emotion. When we make the determination to love, the feelings are a wonderful by-product. Love's lasting is established by often-repeated deeds.

Let us therefore follow after the things which make for peace, and things wherewith one may edify another.
❧ Romans 14:19 ☙

The mighty oak was once a little nut that stood its ground.

34

IN the 1960s, the Federal Drug Administration was receiving nearly 700 applications a year for new medicines. The beleaguered New Drug Section only had sixty days to review each drug before giving its approval or requesting more data.

A few months after Dr. Frances Kelsey joined the FDA, an established pharmaceutical firm in Ohio applied for a license to market a new drug called Kevadon. The drug seemed to relieve nausea in early pregnancy. It was given to millions of expectant women, mostly in Europe, Asia, and Africa. Although scientific studies revealed harmful side effects, the pharmaceutical firm printed leaflets declaring its safety. In anticipation of the drug's approval, the company exerted great pressure on Dr. Kelsey to give permission for labels to be printed.

Dr. Kelsey reviewed the data and said "no." Through several rounds of applications, she continued to find the data unsatisfactory. After a fourteen-month struggle, the company humbly withdrew its application. Kevadon was thalidomide, and by that time, the horror of thalidomide deformities was becoming well publicized! One firm "no" by Dr. Kelsey spared the United States untold agony.

Sometimes standing your ground may not seem that important, but in time you may see the big picture.

A man shall not be established by wickedness:
but the root of the righteous shall not be moved.
▬ Proverbs 12:3 ▬

35

Most people wish to serve God— but only in an advisory capacity.

AN old poem tells the story of a woman who was walking through a meadow one day. As she strolled along meditating on nature, she came upon a field of golden pumpkins. In the corner of the field stood a majestic oak tree.

The woman sat under the oak tree and began musing about the strange twists in nature. Tiny acorns hung on huge branches and huge pumpkins sat on tiny vines. She thought, *God blundered with creation! He should have put the small acorns on the tiny vines and the large pumpkins on the huge branches.*

Before long, the warmth of the autumn sunshine lulled the woman to sleep. She was soon awakened, however, by a tiny acorn bouncing off her nose. Chuckling to herself, she amended her previous thinking, *Maybe God was right after all!*

In every situation, God knows far more about the people and circumstances involved than we can ever know. He alone sees the beginning from the ending. He alone knows how to create a Master Plan that provides for the good of all those who serve Him. Today, trust in Him and His plan—it may seem backwards, but He always does what is best.

Humble yourselves therefore under the mighty hand of God,
that he may exalt you in due time.

᪥ 1 Peter 5:6 ᪥

Most men forget God all day
and ask Him to remember them at night.

MANY people venerate Francis of Assisi, the thirteenth-century saint known for his simple lifestyle and deep love for the poor. During his lifetime, he founded the Franciscan order, restored numerous dilapidated Italian chapels, and helped countless needy people.

What most people don't know, however, is that Francis spent most of his life not in doing good works, but in prayer. St. Bonaventure wrote about him, "Whether walking or sitting, within doors or without, at toil or at leisure, he was so absorbed in prayer that he seemed to have devoted not only his whole heart and body, but also his whole heart and time." Francis regularly set aside hours throughout the day which he called "appointments with God," and he never missed them. On one occasion, as Francis traveled through the large town of Borgo, people pressed in upon him from all sides to touch his garments. Francis was so absorbed in prayer that when he arrived at his destination some time later, he asked when they were going to get to Borgo!

No matter how busy we are, we must never become too busy to pray. Our devotion to God through prayer gives lasting meaning to everything else we undertake.

Evening, and morning, and at noon, will I pray,
and cry aloud: and he shall hear my voice.

Psalm 55:17

*A*lthough the tongue weighs very little, few people are able to hold it.

IDA and David wanted their three sons to graduate from college. Yet they knew their boys would have to pay their own way since David never made more than $150 a month. Still, they encouraged their sons to achieve all they could. Arthur, however, went directly from high school to a job. Edgar began studying law. When Dwight graduated, he didn't have a goal in mind, so he and Ed made a pact: Dwight would work two years while Ed studied, sending Ed as much money as he could, and then they would reverse the arrangement. While he was working though, Dwight found an opportunity that appealed to him more than college—West Point.

Both Ida and David were crushed by Dwight's decision. Ida was deeply convinced that soldiering was wicked. Still, she said, "It is your choice." David also remained silent, allowing his adult son full freedom to forge his own adult future. Yes, Ida and David wisely held their tongues but they never withheld their applause, especially on the day their son, *General* Dwight Eisenhower, became president of the United States of America.

Refraining from giving advice may sometimes be the best gift you could give a person.

Even so the tongue is a little member, and boasteth great things.
Behold, how great a matter a little fire kindleth!
James 3:5

You should never let adversity get you down—except on your knees.

A YOUNG soldier fighting in Italy during World War II managed to jump into a foxhole just ahead of a spray of bullets. He immediately attempted to deepen the hole for more protection. As he was frantically scraping at the dirt with his hands, he unearthed a silver crucifix, obviously left by a previous occupant. A moment later, a leaping figure landed beside him as shells screamed overhead. The soldier turned to see that his new companion was an army chaplain. Holding up the crucifix the soldier cried, "Am I glad to see you! How do you work this thing?"

While flying on a special mission to the Pacific Islands, Captain Eddie Rickenbacker and his crew crashed. They were lost at sea for twenty-one days before being rescued. He said, "In the beginning many of the men were atheists or agnostics, but at the end of the terrible ordeal each, in his own way, had discovered God. Each man found salvation and strength in prayer, and a community of feeling developed which created a liveliness of human fellowship and worship and a sense of gentle peace."

Are you facing a problem today? Begin the search for a solution with prayer.

Is any one of you in trouble? He should pray.
James 5:13 NIV

He who wants milk should not sit on a stool in the middle of the pasture expecting the cow to back up to him.

MISS Jones, an elderly spinster, was the oldest resident of her Midwestern town. When she died, other than noting her age, the editor of the local newspaper was stymied. What could he write in her obituary? Miss Jones had never spent a night in jail or been seen intoxicated on the streets. She had also never done anything good that was worth noting.

While musing about what he might write, the editor went to the local café for coffee, where he met the owner of the tombstone company. He was equally perplexed as to what to write about Miss Jones.

A short time later, the editor returned to his office and assigned both the obituary and tombstone epitaph to the first reporter he saw, who happened to be the sports editor. If you pass through that little town, you'll find this on Miss Jones' tombstone:

> Here lies the bones of Nancy Jones
>
> For her life held no terrors.
>
> She lived an old maid. She died an old maid.
>
> No hits, no runs, no errors.

We each have some contribution to make in life. Give your best effort today. It's your best shot at scoring in the game of life.

He becometh poor that dealeth with a slack hand:
but the hand of the diligent maketh rich.
Proverbs 10:4

$\mathcal{I}$t is good to remember that the teakettle, although up to its neck in hot water, continues to sing.

46

AN old legend tells how a man once stumbled upon a great red barn after wandering for days in a dark, overgrown forest. Seeking refuge from the forest's incessantly howling winds, he gladly entered the barn. When his eyes adjusted to the dark, he discovered to his great astonishment that he was standing in Satan's storehouse of seeds to be sown into human hearts. More curious than fearful, he lit a match and began to explore the seed bins around him. He couldn't help but notice that the containers labeled "discouragement" far outnumbered any other type of seed.

Just as the man had drawn this conclusion, one of Satan's foremost demons arrived to pick up a fresh supply of seed. The man asked him, "Why the great abundance of discouragement seeds?"

"Because they are so effective and they take root so quickly!" the demon laughed. The man then asked, "Do they grow everywhere?" At this the demon became sullen. He glared at the man and admitted in disgust, "No. They never seem to thrive in the heart of a grateful person."

Today, choose to be thankful in every circumstance. Don't let the seeds of discouragement take root in your soul.

Rejoice evermore. In every thing give thanks:
for this is the will of God in Christ Jesus concerning you.
1 Thessalonians 5:16,18

It's good to be a Christian and know it, but it's better to be a Christian and show it!

IN *Les Misérables*, Victor Hugo tells of Jean Valjean, whose only crime was the theft of a loaf of bread to feed his sister's starving children. However, he served nineteen years in prison before being turned out penniless on the streets. Hardened and unable to find work, Valjean finally makes his way to the home of a good old bishop, who gives him supper and a bed for the night. The bishop serves Valjean using his best silver platters and candlesticks.

Yielding to temptation, Valjean steals the bishop's silver platters and slips away, but is soon caught and returned by watchful police. When shown the evidence, the bishop says to the apprehending policeman, "Why, I gave them to him." And then turning to the thief, he adds, "And Jean, you forgot to take the candlesticks." A shocked and eternally grateful Valjean accepts the candlesticks as more than valuable silver pieces, but as expressions of love beyond measure. The bishop's act brought about a true repentance and changed Valjean's life.

Who knows which person might be touched by your act of kindness today. What seems little to you may be great in the eyes of a person in need of love.

By this shall all men know that ye are my disciples,
if ye have love one to another.
John 13:35

$\mathscr{S}$orrow looks back.
Worry looks around.
Faith looks up.

IN *Love and Duty*, Anne Purcell writes about seeing Major Jim Statler standing with her pastor outside his study after a Sunday service. She knew instantly that he was there with news about her husband, Ben, who was on active duty in Vietnam. As she had feared, Jim had a chilling message: "He was on a helicopter that was shot down—he's missing in action."

Anne recalls, "Somewhere in the back of my mind, a little candle flame flickered. This tiny flame was the vestige of my faith." Days passed without word and she found herself able to pray only one thing: "Help me, dear Father." She says, "I hung onto this important truth that He would help me and the flickering flame of my candle of faith began to grow." Then, one day, she noticed a white dove sitting in her yard, a highly uncommon sight in her neighborhood. She took it as a sign from God that He was, indeed, always near.

For five years, Anne Purcell clung to the fact that God was near. Little did she know that her husband was whispering to her from a POW cell, "Anne, find solace and strength in the Lord."

Fixing our eyes on Jesus, the author and perfecter of faith,
who for the joy set before Him endured the cross, despising
the shame, and has sat down at the right hand of
the throne of God.

Hebrews 12:2 NASB

$\mathcal{A}$ man is never in worse company than when he flies into a rage and is beside himself.

A LITTLE girl was once in a very bad mood, so she was taking her frustration out on her younger brother. At first she just teased him, but eventually, she punched him, pulled his hair, and kicked him in the shins. The boy took it all and even dished back a few blows until the kicking began. That hurt! Off he went crying to his mother, complaining about what his sister had done.

The mother came to the little girl and said, "Mary, why have you let Satan put it into your heart to pull your brother's hair and kick his shins?"

The little girl thought it over for a moment and then answered, "Well, Mother, maybe Satan did put it into my heart to pull Tommy's hair, but kicking his shins was my own idea."

All the evil in the world doesn't come from direct satanic involvement. Much of it comes from the heart of man. What we do with our anger and frustrations is subject to our will. We can choose how we will respond to stress, or to the behavior of others. Our challenge is to govern our emotions; otherwise, they will rule in tyranny over us.

He that is soon angry dealeth foolishly.

Proverbs 14:17

$\mathscr{S}$uccess in marriage is more
than finding the right person.
It's becoming the right person.

IN Thornton Wilder's play, *The Skin of Our Teeth*, the character Mrs. Antrobus says to her husband, "I didn't marry you because you were perfect . . . I married you because you gave me a promise."

She then takes off her ring and looks at it, saying, "That promise made up for your faults and the promise I gave you made up for mine. Two imperfect people got married, and it was the promise that made the marriage."

Marriage is indeed a promise. We may at first think our spouse is perfect, but once married we soon realize that's not the case. In every marriage, no matter how well the two people know one another, great mysteries remain! Very often, each person comes to the marriage

—not fully knowing himself or herself,

—not fully knowing about life, and

—not fully knowing about his or her spouse.

What is unknown far outweighs what is known!

Becoming a faithful, loving spouse not only takes courage and faith, but patience and the desire to keep learning and growing. Better than the question, "What kind of spouse do I desire to have?" is the question, "What kind of spouse do I aspire to be?"

But thou, O man of God, flee these things; and follow after righteousness, godliness, faith, love, patience, meekness.

1 Timothy 6:11

*F*alling down doesn't make you a failure, but staying down does.

THOMAS Edison conducted countless experiments with a myriad of materials in search for an effective filament to use in carbon incandescent lamps. As each fiber failed, he would toss it out the window. Ultimately, the pile of failures reached to the second story of his house.

One day in 1879, some thirteen months after he began, he succeeded in finding a filament that would stand the stress of electric current. Here's how: Edison casually picked up a bit of lampblack, mixed it with tar, rolled it into a thin thread, and thought, *Why not try a carbonized cotton fiber?*

He worked for five hours to make a suitable fiber but it broke in two before he removed the mold. He used two spools of cotton thread before a perfect strand emerged, only to be ruined when he tried to place it in a glass tube. He continued without sleep for two days and nights before he managed to slip one of the carbonized threads into a vacuum-sealed bulb. Turning on the current, he saw the glow of electric light that we now take for granted.

A failure doesn't mark the end. It often brings us one step closer to success!

For a just man falleth seven times, and riseth up again.
Proverbs 24:16

*I*f a task is once begun, never leave it 'till it's done. Be the labor great or small, do it well or not at all.

THE order from the head teacher was abrupt: "The classroom needs sweeping. Take the broom and sweep it."

The young man knew this was his chance. He swept the room three times, then dusted four times. When the head teacher came back to evaluate his work, she inspected the floor and then used her handkerchief to rub the woodwork around the walls, the table, and the students' benches. When she could not find one speck of dust anywhere in the room, she said quietly, "I guess you will do to enter this institution."

Cleaning a classroom was nothing less than Booker T. Washington's entrance examination to Hampton Institute in Virginia. In later years, he would recall this as the turning point in his life. He wrote in his autobiography, *Up From Slavery*, "I have passed several examinations since then, but I have always felt that this was the best one I ever passed."

Slacking off, goofing off, and dozing off rarely open doors of opportunity. Those doors are opened best by going above and beyond, by doing more than is required. Whatever your hand finds to do, do it with all your might, and God will bless you with success.

I have glorified thee on the earth: I have finished
the work which thou gavest me to do.

John 17:4

Time is more valuable than money because time is irreplaceable.

HOW many times have we said, or heard others say, "Tomorrow—I'll do it tomorrow." Sometimes people put off doing what they really want to do because they don't think they know enough or can perform well enough. The fact is, there is no magic age at which quality, ability, and excellence emerge.

Thomas Jefferson was thirty-three when he drafted the Declaration of Independence. Benjamin Franklin was twenty-six when he wrote *Poor Richard's Almanac*. Charles Dickens was twenty-four when he began his *Pickwick Papers* and twenty-five when he wrote *Oliver Twist*. Isaac Newton was twenty-four when he formulated the law of gravity.

On the other hand, it is equally wrong to think that creativity and invention belong only to the young. It's just not true! Emmanuel Kant wrote his finest philosophical works at age seventy-four. At eighty, Verdi produced *Falstaff* and at eighty-five, *Ave Maria*. Goethe was eighty when he completed *Faust*. Tennyson was eighty when he wrote *Crossing the Bar* and Michelangelo completed his greatest work at eighty-seven. At the age of ninety, Justice Holmes was still writing brilliant Supreme Court opinions.

Seize the day! Redeem the time now. It's never too early, but it's never too late!

Redeeming the time, because the days are evil.
Ephesians 5:16

The best way to forget
your own problems is to
help someone solve his.

SADHU Sundar Singh and a companion were traveling through a pass high in the Himalayan Mountains when they came across a body lying in the snow. They checked for vital signs and discovered the man was still alive, but barely. Sundar Singh prepared to help this unfortunate traveler, but his companion objected, saying, "We shall lose our lives if we burden ourselves with him." Singh, however, could not think of leaving the man to die in the snow. His companion quickly bade him farewell and walked on.

Sundar Singh lifted the poor traveler onto his back. With great exertion, made even greater by the high altitude and snowy conditions, he carried the man onward. As he walked, the heat cast off by his body began to warm the frozen man. He revived and soon, they were walking together side by side, each holding the other up and keeping the other warm. Before long they came upon another traveler's body lying in the snow. Upon closer inspection, they discovered him to be dead, frozen by the cold.

He was Sundar Singh's original traveling companion.

Don't forget, by reaching out to help others, your own problems are usually forgotten and often solved.

Look not every man on his own things,
but every man also on the things of others.

❧ Philippians 2:4 ☙

*G*od can heal a broken heart,
but He has to have all the pieces.

64

A BOY once said to God, "I know what I want when I grow up." He proceeded to give God his list: to live in a big house with two Saint Bernards; to marry a tall, blue-eyed woman; to have three sons—one who will be a senator, one a scientist, and the other a quarterback. He also wanted to be a mountain climber and drive a red Ferrari.

As it turned out, the boy hurt his knee one day while playing football. He could no longer climb trees, much less mountains. He married a beautiful and kind woman who was short with brown eyes. Because of his business, he lived in an apartment in the city and usually rode the subway. He had three loving daughters, and they adopted a fluffy cat. One daughter became a nurse, one an artist, and the third a music teacher.

One morning the man awoke and remembered his boyhood dream. He became extremely depressed. Heartbroken, he called out to God, "Remember when I was a boy and told You all the things I wanted? Why didn't You give me those things?"

"I could have," said God, "but I wanted to make you happy."

My son, give me thine heart.
Proverbs 23:26

$\mathcal{A}$uthority makes some people grow and others just swell.

EVERYBODY knows of Isaac Newton's famed encounter with a falling apple, and how he introduced the laws of gravity and revolutionized the field of astronomy. But few know that if it weren't for Edmund Halley, the world may never have heard of Newton. Halley challenged Newton to think through his original theories. He corrected Newton's mathematical errors and prepared geometrical figures to support his discoveries. It was Halley who coaxed the hesitant Newton to write his great work, *Mathematical Principles of Natural Philosophy*. And it was Halley who edited and supervised its publication, financing its printing even though Newton was much wealthier.

Historians have called Halley's relationship with Newton one of the most selfless examples in science. As Newton began to reap the rewards of prominence, Halley received little credit. He used the principles Newton developed to predict the orbit of a comet that would later bear his name, but since Halley's Comet only returns every seventy-six years, few hear his name. Still, Halley didn't care who received credit as long as the cause of science was advanced. He was content to live without fame.

The long-term rewards of what we do in life far outweigh the fickleness of recognition.

But he that is greatest among you shall be your servant.
Matthew 23:11

*B*e more concerned with what God
thinks about you than what people
think about you.

DURING her very successful career as an operatic singer, Jenny Lind was known as "The Swedish Nightingale." She became one of the wealthiest artists of her time, yet she left the stage when she was singing her best.

Countless people speculated as to the reason for her leaving, and most people wondered how she could give up so much fame and money. She seemed content, however, to live in privacy in a home by the sea.

One day a friend found her sitting in the sand on the beach, her Bible on her knees, looking out into the glorious glow of a sunset. As they talked, the friend asked, "Madame Goldschmidt, how is it that you ever came to abandon the stage at the height of your success?"

She answered quietly, "When every day it made me think less of this (laying a finger on her Bible) and nothing at all of that (pointing to the sunset), what else could I do?"

The world may never understand your decision to follow God's way. But then, perhaps God cannot understand a decision to pursue what the world offers when He has such great rewards in store for those who follow Him.

Then Peter and the other apostles answered and said,
We ought to obey God rather than men.
Acts 5:29

The trouble with the guy who talks too fast is that he often says something he hasn't thought of yet.

IN 1987, his first full season as manager, Tom Kelly managed the Minnesota Twins to a World Series title. And in 1991, he brought them to a second world championship. Yet to watch him at work, critics have wondered if his vital signs have been stolen. "How has T. K. managed all this, while lowering his blood pressure to the equivalent of the water pressure in your first apartment?" asked one sportswriter. "He doesn't chew on fingernails or Rolaids or tobacco or his players. How?"

One of Kelly's trademarks is that he is a man of few words. He enjoys throwing at batting practice every day, because every minute he is throwing he doesn't have to speak to the media. "I'm not really intelligent," T. K. claims. "I have a year and a half of college. But I have enough common sense to realize that I'm not intelligent. I realize that if I keep talking, I'll eventually say something dumb. So I don't give myself a lot of opportunities to open my mouth and stick my foot in it."

Tom Kelly is far from dumb, and so is any person who thinks before he speaks and keeps his words to a minimum.

Be not rash with thy mouth, and let not thine heart be hasty
to utter any thing before God: for God is in heaven,
and thou upon earth: therefore let thy words be few.

Ecclesiastes 5:2

The train of failure usually runs on the track of laziness.

SUCCESS in business is often closely associated with a person's courage and ability to recover from his or her most recent failure!

In 1928, a thirty-three-year-old man by the name of Paul Galvin, found himself staring at failure—again. He had failed in business twice at this point, his competitors having forced him to fold his latest venture in the storage-battery business. Convinced, however, that he still had a marketable idea, Galvin attended the auction of his own business. With $750 that he had managed to raise, he bought back the battery eliminator portion of the inventory. With it, he built a new company which he succeeded in and eventually retired from, but not before his company became a household word: Motorola. Upon his retirement, Galvin advised others: "Do not fear mistakes. You will know failure—continue to reach out."

A failure isn't truly a failure until you quit trying. If a venture begins to slow down, try speeding up your efforts. Consider the child who allows a bicycle to coast to a halt. Eventually, the bicycle wobbles and the child falls off. The key to avoiding the crash? Faster peddling! The same holds true for many an enterprise. Don't quit trying!

By much slothfulness the building decayeth; and through idleness of the hands the house droppeth through.

Ecclesiastes 10:18

When confronted with a Goliath-sized problem, which way do you respond: "He's too big to hit," or like David, "He's too big to miss"?

ONE day the Pahouins brought a giant native in chains to Albert Schweitzer's hospital. In a fit of madness, N'Tschambi had killed a woman. Reaching down to help the man to the landing, Schweitzer saw fear and sadness in his face. When others refused his order to remove the man's chains, he did it himself. He then explained sedatives to N'Tschambi, and the fearful man gratefully accepted them. That night he slept without nightmares for the first time.

N'Tschambi became a model patient and soon Schweitzer gave him periods of freedom outside his room, to which he returned voluntarily if he became agitated. Still, he tackled any task he was given with such a fierce energy that he frightened the staff. One day Schweitzer gave him an axe and asked him to help him make a clearing. N'Tschambi was afraid to touch the axe for fear of what he might do with it. Schweitzer said, "If I'm not afraid, why should you be?" The two walked off into the jungle. Hours later, they returned, N'Tschambi's big body dripping with sweat but a radiant smile on his lips. The giant inside had been transformed by the kindness and faith of another human being.

The LORD that delivered me out of the paw of the lion,
and out of the paw of the bear, he will deliver me
out of the hand of this Philistine.
1 Samuel 17:37

*F*orget yourself for others, and others will not forget you!

REPORTERS and city officials gathered at a Chicago railroad station one afternoon in 1953. They were anxiously awaiting the arrival of the 1952 Nobel Peace Prize winner. A few minutes after the train came to a stop, a giant of a man— six-feet-four with bushy hair and a large moustache—stepped from the train. Cameras flashed. City officials approached him with outstretched hands. Various ones began telling him how honored they were to meet him.

The man politely thanked them and then looking over their heads, asked if he could be excused for a moment. He quickly made his way through the crowd until he reached the side of an elderly black woman who was struggling with two large suitcases. He picked up the bags and escorted the woman to a bus. After helping her aboard, he wished her a safe journey. Returning to the greeting party he apologized, "Sorry to have kept you waiting."

The man was Dr. Albert Schweitzer, the famous missionary doctor who had spent his life helping the poor in Africa. In response to Schweitzer's action, one member of the reception committee said with great admiration, "That's the first time I ever saw a sermon walking."

Therefore all things whatsoever ye would that men should do to you, do ye even so to them: for this is the law and the prophets.
₨ Matthew 7:12 ₨

The secret of contentment is the realization that life is a gift, not a right.

AT age fourteen, Andrea Jaeger won her first professional tennis tournament. At eighteen, she reached the finals of Wimbledon. At nineteen, a bad shoulder all but ended her career. Many a world-class athlete may have become bitter or discontented with life at that point. However, Jaeger turned her competitive spirit to a new endeavor, a nonprofit organization called Kids' Stuff Foundation. The foundation attempts to bring joy to children suffering from cancer and other life-threatening illnesses. Her work there has also inspired her to take correspondence studies in nursing and child psychology.

Jaeger not only created the program, but runs it full-time, year-round, unpaid. "I'm inspired by these brave kids, and humbled," she has said. "They lose their health, their friends, and sometimes their lives. And yet their spirit never wavers. They look at life as a gift. The rest of us sometimes look at ourselves as a gift to life.

"You get very spoiled on the tour," she adds with a twinkle in her eye. "The courtesy cars, the five-star hotels, the thousands of people clapping for you when you hit a good shot. It's easy to forget what's important in life. I forget it a lot less lately."

But godliness with contentment is great gain.

1 Timothy 6:6

True faith and courage are
like a kite—an opposing
wind raises it higher.

NORMA Zimmer, the well-known Lawrence Welk singer, had a difficult childhood as a result of her parents' drinking. Singing was her escape. As a high school senior, Norma was invited to sing at the University Christian Church in Seattle. When her parents heard she was going to sing a particular song, they insisted on attending the service. She tells about that morning, "I stole glances at the congregation, trying to find my parents . . . then in horror I saw them weaving down the aisle in a state of disheveled intoxication. They were late. Few empty seats were left. The congregation stared. I don't know how I ever got through that morning."

After she sang and took her seat, the pastor preached: "God is our refuge and strength, a tested help in time of trouble." She says, "My own trouble seemed to bear down on me with tremendous weight. . . . I realized how desperate life in our family was without God, and that day I recommitted my life to Him. Jesus came into my life not only as Savior but for daily strength and direction."

Don't let a difficult time box you in. Let it drive you to Jesus.

But they that wait upon the LORD shall renew their strength;
they shall mount up with wings as eagles; they shall run,
and not be weary; and they shall walk, and not faint.

Isaiah 40:31

$\mathcal{T}$hose who bring sunshine to the lives of others cannot keep it from themselves.

THE story is told of a man and woman who gave a sizeable contribution to their church to honor the memory of their son who lost his life in the war. When the announcement of their generous donation was made to the congregation, a woman whispered to her husband, "Let's give the same amount in honor of each of our boys."

The husband replied, "What are you talking about? Neither one of our sons was killed in the war."

"Exactly," said the woman. "Let's give it as an expression of our gratitude to God for sparing their lives!"

What we give during our life produces benefits in three ways: (1) it helps those in need; (2) it inspires others to give; and, (3) it forms within us an inner character marked not by selfishness and materialism, but by generosity and gratitude.

When you give, keep in mind the people your gift will ultimately reach. Your church and the charitable organizations you may give to are made up of people. The Bible tells us that whatever a man sows, he will reap. Your giving brings sunshine to the lives of others, and it will be multiplied back to you.

Be not deceived; God is not mocked: for whatsoever a man soweth, that shall he also reap.

Galatians 6:7

*N*o man ever really finds out what he believes in until he begins to instruct his children.

84

A DOG wandered to a preacher's home, and his three sons quickly became quite fond of him. It so happened that the dog had three white hairs in its tail. One day, the preacher and his sons spotted an advertisement about a lost dog. The description matched the stray perfectly.

The minister said, "In the presence of my three boys, we carefully separated the three white hairs and removed them from the dog's tail."

The owner of the dog eventually discovered where his pooch had gone and came to claim him. The dog showed every sign of recognizing his owner, so the man was ready to take him. At that point, the minister spoke up and asked, "Didn't you say the dog would be known by three white hairs in its tail?" The owner, unable to find the hairs, was forced to admit this dog didn't fully fit the description, and he left.

Years passed and the minister noted with sadness, "We kept the dog, but I lost my three boys for Christ that day."

Remember, your children watch the choices you make in all areas of your life. Model Christ before them and they will become models of Christ.

And, ye fathers, provoke not your children to wrath:
but bring them up in the nurture and admonition of the Lord.
Ephesians 6:4

It's the little things in life that
determine the big things.

SEVERAL centuries ago, the Emperor of Japan commissioned a Japanese artist to paint a particular species of bird for him. Months passed, then years. Finally, the Emperor himself went to the artist's studio to ask for an explanation.

The artist set a blank canvas on the easel and within fifteen minutes, had completed an incredible painting of the bird. It was a masterpiece! Admiring both the painting and the artist's great skill, the Emperor couldn't understand why there had been such a long delay.

Without speaking a word, the artist went from cabinet to cabinet in his studio. He pulled out armloads of drawings of feathers, tendons, wings, feet, claws, eyes, beaks—virtually every aspect of a bird, from virtually every angle. He placed these before the Emperor, who nodded in understanding. The magnificence of any finished product can never be greater than the magnificence of any singular detail.

To have an excellent life, strive for an excellent year. Within that year, strive for an excellent month; within that month, strive for an excellent day. Within a day, strive for an excellent hour; within an hour, strive for excellent minutes. An excellent life is the sum of many excellent moments!

Thou hast been faithful over a few things, I will make thee ruler over many things: enter thou into the joy of thy lord.
Matthew 25:21

The doors of opportunity are marked "Push" and "Pull."

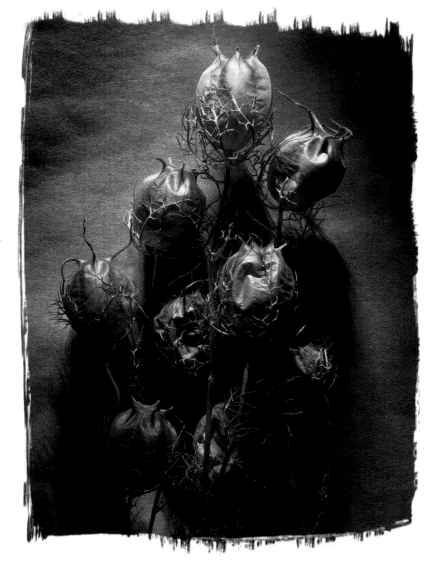

A MAN once went for a ride in the country with a friend. They drove off the main road and through a grove of orange trees to a mostly uninhabited piece of land. Walter stopped the car and began to vividly describe the things he was going to build on the land. He explained to his friend, "I can handle the main project myself. It will take all my money, but I want you to have the first chance at this surrounding acreage, because in the next five years it will increase in value several hundred times."

Arthur thought to himself, *Who in the world is going to drive twenty-five miles for this crazy project? His dream has taken the best of his common sense.* He promised to look into the deal later. "Later on will be too late," Walter cautioned. "You'd better move on it right now." Arthur failed to act, however.

And so it was that Art Linkletter turned down the opportunity to buy the land that surrounded what would become Disneyland, the land his friend Walt Disney had tried to talk him into buying.

When opportunity greets you, sometimes you have to take a step of faith.

The soul of the sluggard desireth, and hath nothing: but the soul of the diligent shall be made fat.

Proverbs 13:4

$\mathcal{T}$he best way to be successful is to follow the advice you give others.

AN officer in the navy had dreamed from childhood of commanding a great battleship one day. When he finally achieved his dream, he was given commission of the newest and proudest ship in the fleet.

One stormy night, the captain was on duty on the bridge when he spotted a strange light rapidly closing on his own vessel. As his ship plowed through the giant waves, the light rose and fell just above the horizon of the sea. He ordered his signalman to flash a message to the unidentified craft on his port side, "Alter your course ten degrees to the south."

Within seconds a reply came back, "Alter your course ten degrees to the north." Determined that his ship would never take a backseat to any other, the captain snapped a second order, "Alter your course ten degrees—I am the Captain!" The response was beamed back, "Alter your course ten degrees I am Seaman Third Class Smith." By this time the light was growing ever brighter and larger.

Infuriated, the captain grabbed the signal light and personally signaled, "Alter your course. I am a battleship." The reply came just as quickly, "Alter your course. I am a lighthouse."

He who ignores discipline despises himself,
but whoever heeds correction gains understanding.
Proverbs 15:32 NIV

*C*ontentment isn't getting what
we want but being satisfied
with what we have.

THE story is told of a farmer who had lived on the same farm all his life. It was a good farm with fertile soil, but as the years passed, the farmer began to think, *Maybe there's something better for me.* He set out to find an even better plot of land.

Every day he found a new reason for criticizing his old farm. Finally, he decided to sell. He listed the farm with a real estate broker who promptly prepared an advertisement emphasizing the many advantages of the acreage: ideal location, modern equipment, healthy stock, acres of fertile ground, high yielding crops, well-kept barns and pens, and a nice two-story house on a hill above the pasture.

The real estate agent called the farmer to read the ad to him prior to placing it in the local paper. When he had finished, the farmer cried, "Hold everything! I've changed my mind. I've been looking for a place just like that all my life!"

When you start identifying the good traits of any person, situation, or organization, you are likely to find that they far outweigh the bad. Focus on what you have, and what you don't have will seem insignificant.

Not that I speak in respect of want: for I have learned,
in whatsoever state I am, therewith to be content.

Philippians 4:11

Too many people quit looking for work when they find a job.

IN her autobiography, *Who Could Ask for Anything More*, Ethel Merman tells how Cole Porter and a buddy of his had a game they played with Irving Berlin. Says Merman, "When they see Irving coming they look at their wristwatches and make a five-dollar bet. Then they pick a topic and start in on it. Anything will do. The bet is based on the number of minutes it will take Irving to bring the conversation around to one of his songs, no matter where it starts. The average time is said to be less than five minutes."

Merman notes, "I wouldn't go so far as to call this ego on Irving's part. It's just that he's so absorbed in his work and so intense about it that what he writes is the most important thing in the world to him. To me, he doesn't seem so much egotistical as enthusiastic."

It's interesting that Cole Porter would play such a trick since he once told an interviewer, "If I don't seem to be listening to what you're saying, it's because I'm writing a song in the back of my head. Some people think work is a four-letter word. I don't."

He also that is slothful in his work is brother to him
that is a great waster.
Proverbs 18:9

*A*bility will enable a man to go to the top, but it takes character to keep him there.

CONVICTED Watergate conspirator John Ehrlichman wrote of his experience: "When I went to jail . . . I had a big self-esteem problem. I was a felon, shorn and scorned. . . . I wondered if anyone thought I was worth anything. . . . For years I had been able to sweep most of my shortcomings and failures under the rug and not face them, but during the two long criminal trials, I spent my days listening to prosecutors tell juries what a bad fellow I was. I'd go back to a hotel room and sit alone thinking about what was happening to me. During that time I began to take stock.

"I was wiped out. I had nothing left that had been of value to me."

Then he began to see himself and to care about his integrity, his capacity to love and be loved. He concluded about the Nixon years, "In a paradoxical way, I'm grateful for them. Somehow I had to see all of that and grow to understand it in order to arrive."

Keep a daily check on your character. Of all the abilities you may possess, the ability to develop good character is your greatest.

The righteousness of the blameless makes a straight way for them,
but the wicked are brought down by their own wickedness.
Proverbs 11:5 NIV

Your words are windows to your heart.

AUTHOR J. Allan Petersen tells about a flight he took on a 747 out of Brazil. He was awakened by a voice announcing, "We have a very serious emergency." Three engines had quit because of fuel contamination and the fourth was expected to go at any second. They began to prepare for an emergency landing.

At first the situation seemed unreal to Petersen, but when the steward barked, "Prepare for impact," he found himself and everyone around him praying. As he buried his head in his lap and pulled up his knees, he said, "Oh, God, thank You. Thank You for the incredible privilege of knowing You. Life has been wonderful." As the plane approached the ground, his last cry was, "Oh, God, my wife! My children!"

Petersen survived. As he wandered about the airport in a daze, he found he couldn't speak, but his mind was racing, *What were my last words? What was the bottom line?* Then he remembered: relationship. Reunited with his wife and sons, he found that all he could say to them over and over was, "I appreciate you, I appreciate you!"

Have you told the people who matter most to you how you feel?

For out of the abundance of the heart the mouth speaketh.
Matthew 12:34

A shut mouth gathers no foot.

CONSTANCE Cameron tells of a lesson her mother once taught her. One day, when she was about eight, she was playing outside next to an open window. Inside, Mrs. Brown was confiding a personal problem to Constance's mother. After Mrs. Brown had gone, the mother realized that Constance had heard everything that had been said. She called her in and said, "If Mrs. Brown had left her purse here today, would we give it to anyone else?"

"Of course not," the girl said. Her mother went on, "Mrs. Brown left something more precious than her pocketbook today. She left a story that could make many people unhappy. That story is not ours to give to anyone. It is still hers, even though she left it here. So we shall not give it to anyone. Do you understand?"

She did. And from that day on, whenever a friend would share a confidence or even engage in careless gossip, she considered what they said to be their personal property and not hers to give to anyone else.

This old saying bears great truth: "If you don't have something good to say about someone or something, don't say anything at all."

He that keepeth his mouth keepeth his life:
but he that openeth wide his lips shall have destruction.
Proverbs 13:3

The only fool bigger than the person who knows it all is the person who argues with him.

WHEN Charles Spurgeon was still a young preacher, he was warned about a certain woman with a reputation for being extremely quarrelsome. He was told that she intended to give him a tongue-lashing the next time she saw him.

Spurgeon said, "All right, but that's a game two can play." Shortly thereafter she met him and began to assault him with a flood of verbal abuse. He simply smiled back at her and said, "Oh, yes, thank you. I am quite well. Thank you for asking. I hope you are the same."

His remarks were followed by another tirade of know-it-all comments, this time voiced at a slightly higher volume. He responded again, smiling quietly, "Yes, it does look rather as if it might rain. I think I had better be getting on."

"Bless the man!" the woman exclaimed and then concluded, "He's as deaf as a post. What's the use of storming at him!"

Never again did she assault Spurgeon with her arguments. And never did he tell her what he had done! There's no point in arguing with know-it-all people. It's better to let them have their say and walk on.

He that reproveth a scorner getteth to himself shame: and
he that rebuketh a wicked man getteth himself a blot.

Proverbs 9:7

*B*lessed is he who, having nothing to say, refrains from giving wordy evidence of the fact.

IN the eighteenth century, Dr. Johann Beringer was a professor of natural philosophy at the University of Wurzburg, Germany. He concluded that fossils were not linked to previously living animals, as some were advocating, but that they were unique creations, each part of a divine message planted into the earth by the Lord at the time of creation. He advocated that man study the fossils with the intent of uncovering the meaning of God's buried message.

His students decided to make and then implant into a nearby hillside, hundreds of grotesque clay forms, some fossil-like and others with writing on them. One of the clay figures was actually signed by "Jehovah."

The doctor was so convinced that his "find" had divine meaning that he published a book on the subject, ignoring the repeated confessions of his students. He chided his students for attempting to undermine his work and rob him of the fame due him. It was not until Beringer discovered a "fossil" bearing his own name that he accepted the hoax for what it had been. And for the rest of his life, he spent a small fortune trying to buy back the existing copies of his own book.

The tongue of the wise useth knowledge aright:
but the mouth of fools poureth out foolishness.
Proverbs 15:2

Luck:
a loser's excuse for a winner's position.

DURING the reign of Abdullah the Third, a great drought struck Baghdad. The Mohammendan doctors issued a decree that all the faithful should offer prayers for rain. Still, the drought continued. The Jews were then permitted to add their prayers. Their supplications also appeared ineffectual. Finally when the drought resulted in widespread famine, the Christians in the land were asked to pray. It so happened that torrents of rain followed almost immediately.

The whole Conclave was more upset over the cessation of the drought than it had been alarmed at its continuance. They couldn't let people think the prayers of the Christians had been fruitful. Feeling that some explanation was necessary, they issued this statement to the masses: "The God of our Prophet was highly gratified by the prayers of the faithful which were as sweet-smelling savors to Him. He refused their requests in order to prolong the pleasure of listening to their prayers; but the prayers of those Christian infidels were an abomination to Him, and He granted their petitions the sooner to be rid of their loathsome importunities."

Be careful how you ridicule a victor. He may have the skill to beset you again in yet another contest.

The soul of the sluggard desireth, and hath nothing: but the soul of the diligent shall be made fat.
Proverbs 13:4

*D*o the thing you fear, and the
death of fear is certain.

ON a summer morning as he was fixing his breakfast, Ray Blankenship looked out his kitchen window to see a young girl being swept along in the rain-flooded drainage ditch beside his Ohio home. Blankenship knew that farther downstream, the ditch disappeared underneath the road with a roar and then emptied into the main culvert.

Ray dashed from his home and raced along the ditch, frantically trying to get ahead of the flailing child. Finally, he hurled himself into the deep, churning water. When he surfaced, he was able to grab the girl's arm. The two tumbled end over end and then, within about three feet of the yawning culvert, Ray's free hand felt something protruding from the bank. He clung to it desperately, the tremendous force of the water trying to tear him and the child away to be sucked under the road.

Amazingly, by the time the fire department rescuers arrived Blankenship had pulled the girl to safety. Both were treated for shock. In that heroic moment, Ray Blankenship was at even greater risk than most people knew—since Ray couldn't swim.

Respond in courage to the needs you see, rather than retreating in the fear you may feel.

Be strong and of a good courage, fear not, nor be afraid of them:
for the LORD thy God, he it is that doth go with thee;
he will not fail thee, nor forsake thee.
Deuteronomy 31:6

God plus one is always a majority!

WISHING to encourage her young son's progress at the piano, a mother bought tickets to an Ignace Paderewski performance. When the night arrived, the two found their seats near the front of the concert hall. The boy stared in wide-eyed amazement at the majestic grand piano on the stage. The mother began talking to a friend and she failed to notice her son slip away. As the house lights dimmed and the spotlight hit the piano, the woman gasped as she saw her son at the piano bench, picking out "Twinkle, Twinkle, Little Star."

Before the woman could retrieve her son, the famous concert pianist appeared on stage and quickly moved to the keyboard. "Don't quit, keep playing," he whispered to the boy. Leaning over, Paderewski reached down with his left hand and began filling in a bass part. Then with his right arm, he reached around the other side, encircling the child, to add a running obligato. Together, the old master and the young novice mesmerized the crowd.

No matter how insignificant you may feel today, God has these words for you, "Don't quit, keep playing." He will add whatever is needed to turn your efforts into a masterpiece.

If God be for us, who can be against us?

Romans 8:31

Whoever gossips to you will be a gossip of you.

IN 1752, a group of Methodist men, including John Wesley, signed a covenant which every man agreed to hang on his study wall. The six articles of this solemn agreement were as follows:

1. That we will not listen or willingly inquire after ill concerning one another;
2. That, if we do hear any ill of each other, we will not be forward to believe it;
3. That as soon as possible we will communicate what we hear by speaking or writing to the person concerned;
4. That until we have done this, we will not write or speak a syllable of it to any other person;
5. That neither will we mention it, after we have done this, to any other person;
6. That we will not make any exception to any of these rules unless we think ourselves absolutely obliged.

Talk about an Anti-Gossip Pact! Those seven men knew the truth about gossip. Gossip destroys relationships, organizations, churches, and ultimately lives. There is nothing beneficial about gossip; it must be avoided.

Be careful who you confide in. Always remember: the person who tells you "don't tell this to a soul" has probably told all the souls you know.

A talebearer revealeth secrets: but he that is of
a faithful spirit concealeth the matter.
❧ Proverbs 11:13 ☙

*E*very person should have a special
cemetery lot in which to bury the faults
of friends and loved ones.

AN old legend tells of a covey of quail that lived in a forest. They would have been happy except for their enemy, the quail catcher. He would imitate their call, and then when they gathered together, he would throw a net over them and carry them off to market.

One wise quail said, "Brothers, I have a plan. When the fowler puts his net over us, we should each put our head into a section of the net and begin to flap our wings. We can lift the net together and fly away with it." All agreed. The next day, they did just that, making a successful escape. After several days, the fowler's wife asked him, "Where are the quail to take to market?" He replied, "All the birds work together and help one another escape."

Awhile later, one quail began to fight with another. "I lifted all the weight on the net. You didn't help at all," he cried. The other quail became angry and before long, the entire covey was quarreling. The fowler saw his chance. Preoccupied with their quarreling, they didn't help one another.

Pointing out the faults of others can do us in as well.

And be ye kind one to another, tenderhearted,
forgiving one another, even as God for
Christ's sake hath forgiven you.
Ephesians 4:32

Ignorance is always swift to speak.

ONE of the favorite stories of Arturo Toscanini, the great symphony conductor, was this: An orchestra was rehearsing Beethoven's *Leonore* overture, which has two great musical climaxes. Each of these musical high points is followed by a trumpet passage, which the composer intended to be played offstage.

When the first climax arrived, no sound came from the trumpet offstage. The conductor, annoyed, went on to the second musical high point. But again no trumpet could be heard.

This time, the conductor rushed into the wings, fuming. He intended to demand a full explanation. There he found the trumpet player struggling with the house security man who was insisting as he held for dear life onto the man's trumpet, "I tell you, you can't play that trumpet back here! You'll disturb the rehearsals!"

Both the conductor and the security guard were wrong: The conductor, for assuming the trumpet player was asleep on the job; and the security guard for assuming the trumpet player was a rogue. Until you know why someone is acting the way they are, it's better not to criticize him. In addition, until you know who has told someone to act, it's better not to attempt to stop him!

Let every man be swift to hear, slow to speak, slow to wrath.
James 1:19

*P*ick your friends but not to pieces.

AN army trumpeter was once captured by the enemy. He pleaded with his captors: "Please spare me! I have not killed a single one of your soldiers. I only carry this poor brass trumpet and play it when I'm told to."

"That is the very reason for putting you to death," his captors said. "For, while you do not fight yourself, your trumpet stirs up all the others to battle!"

So it is with our criticism of others. We may not hate, mistrust, or avoid the person we criticize, but our criticism can cause others to manifest these feelings and behaviors.

There once was a woman to whom criticism was so distasteful that whenever a visitor brought up something negative about a person, she would say, "Come, let's go and ask if this is true." The talebearer was always so taken aback that she would beg to be excused. But the determined woman would insist on escorting the reluctant soul to the subject of the tale to hear the other point of view. After awhile, no one repeated a tale or criticism in her presence!

When speaking to or about a friend, stir up life instead of strife.

*A man that beareth false witness against his neighbour is
a maul, and a sword, and a sharp arrow.*

Proverbs 25:18

*H*e who throws dirt loses ground.

R. G. LeTourneau, the outstanding Christian businessman for whom LeTourneau College was named, made a fortune with a company that manufactured large earthmoving equipment. He once remarked, "We used to make a scraper known as 'Model G.' One day somebody asked our salesman what the G stood for. The man, who was pretty quick on the trigger, immediately replied, 'I'll tell you. The G stands for gossip because like a talebearer, this machine moves a lot of dirt and moves it fast.'"

The trouble with gossip is not so much that it is spoken as an intentional lie, but that it is heard as if it was the absolute truth. Abraham Lincoln had a favorite riddle he used to pose to people: "If a man were to call the tail of a dog a leg, how many legs would the dog have?"

The usual reply was, "five."

"Wrong," Lincoln would say with his wry smile. "The dog still has four legs. Calling the tail a leg doesn't make it one."

Just because a tale may have been repeated many times by so-called reliable sources, that doesn't necessarily make it true. Build people up by leaving the dirt where it belongs.

*Wherefore putting away lying, speak every man truth with
his neighbour: for we are members one of another.*
Ephesians 4:25

The greatest possession you have is the twenty-four hours directly in front of you.

DR. C. C. Albertson once wrote this about the use of time: "It might be wise for us to take a little inventory of our resources as to time and review our habits of using it. There are 168 hours in each week. Fifty-six of these we spend in sleep. Of the remaining 112 hours, we devote 48 to labor. This leaves 64 hours, of which let us assign 12 hours for our daily meals.

"We have left 52 hours, net, of conscious, active life to devote to any purpose to which we are inclined.

"Is it too much to say that God requires a tithe of this free time? One tenth of 52 hours is 5.2 hours. How much of this tithe of time do we devote to strictly religious uses?"

If one allowed an hour for church attendance and an hour for a Bible study or prayer meeting each week, he would still have 192 minutes a week—enough for nearly a half hour each day in prayer and Bible reading.

From that perspective the excuse, "I have too little time," doesn't fly. What is more likely the case is too little planning of the time we have!

For there is a time there for every purpose and for every work.

Ecclesiastes 3:17

he most valuable gift you can give another is a good example.

IN his autobiography Armand Hammer, known as much for his humanitarian efforts as for his tremendous business pursuits, reveals the roots of his giving spirit:

"My father had become a prominent and greatly loved figure in the area. It was an almost ecstatic experience for me to ride with him when he went on his doctor's rounds . . . patients at their doors greeted him with such warmth that waves of pride and honor would surge in me to find myself the son of such a father, a man so good . . . so obviously deserving of the affection he received.

"He could have made himself many times richer, however, if he had insisted on collecting all his bills. . . . I have seen, in his office, drawers full of unpaid bills for which he refused to demand payment because he knew the difficult circumstances of the patients. And I heard innumerable stories from patients about his leaving money behind to pay for the prescriptions he had written when he visited people who were too poor to eat, let alone pay the doctor."

What a wonderful legacy to leave your child, the "business" of loving and giving to others.

For I have given you an example,
that ye should do as I have done to you.
ș John 13:15 Ș

Don't be afraid of pressure.
Remember that pressure is
what turns a lump of coal
into a diamond.

AN old legend says that God first created birds without wings. Sometime later, God made wings and said to the birds, "Come, take up these burdens and bear them." The birds hesitated at first but soon obeyed. They tried picking up the wings in their beaks, but they were too heavy. Then they tried picking them up with their claws, but they were too large. Finally, one of the birds managed to hoist the wings onto its shoulders where it was possible to carry them.

Before long the wings began to grow and they soon had attached themselves to the birds' bodies. One of the birds began to flap his wings, and others followed his example. Before long, one of the birds took off and began to soar in the air above!

What had once been a heavy burden now became the very thing that enabled the birds to go where they could never go before and at the same time, truly fulfill the destiny of their creation.

The duties and responsibilities you count as burdens today may be part of God's destiny for your life, the means by which your soul will be lifted up and prepared for eternity.

Knowing this, that the trying of your faith worketh patience.

James 1:3

A minute of thought is worth more than an hour of talk.

WHEN William Gladstone was chancellor of the Exchequer, he once requested that the Treasury send him certain statistics upon which he might base his budget proposals. The statistician made a mistake. But Gladstone was so certain of this man's concern for accuracy that he didn't verify the figures. As a result, he went before the House of Commons and made a speech based upon the incorrect figures. His speech was no sooner published than the inaccuracies were exposed, and Gladstone became the brunt of public ridicule.

The chancellor sent for the statistician who had given him the erroneous information. The man arrived full of fear and shame, certain he was going to be let go. Instead, Gladstone said, "I know how much you must be disturbed over what has happened, and I have sent for you to put you at your ease. For a long time you have been engaged in handling the intricacies of the national accounts, and this is the first mistake that you have made. I want to congratulate you, and express to you my keen appreciation."

It takes a big person to extend mercy, to listen rather than talk, and to think before jumping into action.

Set a watch, O LORD, before my mouth; keep the door of my lips.
Psalm 141:3

You can win more friends with
your ears than with your mouth.

RABBI Harold S. Kushner writes in *When All You've Ever Wanted Isn't Enough:*

"A business associate of my father's died under tragic circumstances, and I accompanied my father to the funeral. The man's widow and children were surrounded by clergy and psychiatrists trying to ease their grief. They knew all the right words, but nothing helped. The widow kept saying, 'You're right, I know you're right, but it doesn't make any difference.'

"Then a man walked in, a burly man who was a legend in the toy and game industry. He had come to this country illiterate and penniless and had built up an immensely successful company. He was known as hard and ruthless. Despite his success, he had never learned to read or write. . . . He had been sick recently, and his face and his walking showed it. But he walked over to the widow and started to cry, and she cried with him, and you could feel the atmosphere in the room change. This man who had never read a book in his life spoke the language of the heart and held the key that opened the gates of solace where learned doctors and clergy could not."

When words are many, sin is not absent,
but he who holds his tongue is wise.
Proverbs 10:19 NIV

*R*eputation is made in a moment; character is built in a lifetime.

A MAN once had a friend who was a skilled potter. He often enjoyed watching him at work. One day he asked his friend how he determined what he was going to make. The potter said he had discovered that when he was rested, he tended to make beautiful things, but when he was tired, he made more ordinary vessels. As the potter reflected on this, he concluded that when he was relaxed, he had both the ability to focus and the patience to make something beautiful.

Oftentimes the process of making a perfect object involved crushing an almost completed vase or bowl back into a lump so that he might start over. Beautiful objects also required that he be much more focused. When he was tired, he was less able to focus, less patient, and thus more apt to make mistakes.

So it is with our lives. Building character takes focus and patience, with attention to detail and an ability to be consistent over time. While God is the Master Potter, we also play the role of potter in forming our own character. The more relaxed we are, the more likely we are to create a character of beauty.

My righteousness I hold fast, and will not let it go:
my heart shall not reproach me so long as I live.
Job 27:6

*I*f you feel "dog tired" at night,
maybe it's because you "growled" all day.

GENERAL Horace Porter once wrote about a conversation he had with General Ulysses Grant. Porter noted, "General, it seems singular that you should have gone through all the rough and tumble of army service and frontier life, and have never been provoked into swearing. I have never heard you utter an oath."

Grant replied, "Well, somehow or other, I never learned to swear. When a boy, I seemed to have an aversion to it, and when I became a man I saw the folly of it. I have always noticed, too, that swearing helps to arouse a man's anger; and when a man flies into a passion, his adversary who keeps cool always gets the better of him. In fact, I could never see the value of swearing. I think it is the case with many people who swear excessively that it is a mere habit . . . they do not mean to be profane; to say the least, it is a great waste of time."

Not only does anger give rise to harsh words, but harsh words feed anger. To rid yourself of feelings of anger and frustration, perhaps the first step is to watch your tongue!

If it be possible, as much as lieth in you,
live peaceably with all men.
Romans 12:18

Our children are like mirrors— they reflect our attitudes in life.

SEVERAL years ago, a man was asked to give a commencement address at a local college. As he sat on the platform after his speech watching the graduates receive their degrees, the entire audience began applauding for a student who had earned a perfect 4.0 grade point average. During the applause, a faculty member seated next to the speaker leaned over and said to him, "She may be Miss Genius, but her attitude stinks." The speaker later said, "Without even thinking, my hands stopped clapping for her in midair. I couldn't help but think, *How sad.*"

No matter how beautiful, intelligent, talented, or athletic a child may be there's no substitute for having a positive, generous, and loving attitude toward others! The foremost architect of that attitude is not a child's teacher or pastor, but his or her parents.

Be watchful of the attitudes you feed your children each day. They are the nourishment of your child's mind, just as food is nourishment for your child's body. Don't feed your children junk ideas, sour opinions, rotten theology, poisoned feelings, or wilted enthusiasm. Instead, feed your children with the best ideas, positive opinions, generous feelings, and freshest enthusiasm you can muster!

The just man walketh in his integrity:
his children are blessed after him.
Proverbs 20:7

*H*e who cannot forgive breaks
the bridge over which he himself
must pass.

ONE Sunday afternoon, Doris Louise Seger opened the door of her church office to practice the violin, only to find her violin scattered across the floor in pieces. Doris was crushed. She had received the violin fifty years earlier as a high school graduation present from her parents. She thought, *Who? Why? How can I forgive this person?*

A week later, police found the vandal, and Doris went to his home. When she saw the skinny, blond eleven-year-old, she understood that the real tragedy was not her shattered violin, but a young life headed for a shattered future. She found herself saying, "I forgive you, and God will, too, if you ask Him."

A few days later, the boy came to the pastor's office, asking hesitantly, "Is there any work I can do at the church to pay for the violin?" At the sign of his repentant heart, the pastor shared the Gospel with him, and the boy received Jesus as his Savior that day.

Doris purchased a new violin, but as she later wrote, "It would never compare with this 'new creature' in Christ Jesus. I learned anew that God's grace is sufficient to give me a forgiving heart."

For if ye forgive men their trespasses,
your heavenly Father will also forgive you.
Matthew 6:14

*J*esus is a friend who walks in
when the world has walked out.

BABE Ruth hit 714 home runs during his baseball career, but on this particular day, the Braves were playing the Reds in Cincinnati, and the great Bambino was no hero. In one inning alone, his errors were responsible for most of the five runs scored by Cincinnati.

As Babe walked off the field and headed toward the dugout after the third out, a crescendo of boos rose to greet him. Then, a boy jumped over the railing and ran out onto the field. With tears streaming down his face, he threw his arms around the legs of his hero.

Ruth immediately picked the boy up, hugged him, then set him down and patted his head. The cries from the crowd abruptly stopped. A hush fell over the entire park. In that brief moment, the fans saw two heroes on the field: Ruth, who, in spite of his own dismal day, cared about the feelings of a young fan; and a small boy, who cared about the feelings of another human being.

Regardless of your performance on the playing field of life today, Father God has a hug awaiting you at the day's end. He is your Number One Fan.

These things I have spoken unto you, that in me ye
might have peace. In the world ye shall have tribulation:
but be of good cheer; I have overcome the world.
John 16:33

*F*aith is daring the soul to go beyond what the eyes can see.

142

DURING his time in the army, David Brenner made the most of his duty in Europe by traveling at every opportunity. He often showed up at a train station and bought a ticket to wherever the next train was going.

One day he bought a ticket for Rome and since the train was scheduled to leave immediately, he raced across the station, but still arrived at the track just as the train was pulling away. He chased after it as fast as he could run! Standing on the platform of the last car was a well-dressed man who motioned for him to hand him his bags. He quickly tossed them to him, but then he looked into the man's face! The smirk he saw quickly told him that the man had offered his help not altruistically, but criminally. If Brenner didn't make it on board, this man had brand-new clothes and gear!

Brenner kicked up his heels and running as never before, he managed to grab the railing of the last car. With all the strength he could muster, he swung himself aboard.

Adversity sometimes comes to rob you. Instead, let it motivate your faith to be even more daring!

For we walk by faith, not by sight.

2 Corinthians 5:7

The fellow who does things
that count doesn't usually
stop to count them.

FOR more than a quarter of a century, Arnold Billie was a rural mail carrier in southern New Jersey. His daily route took him sixty-three miles through two counties and five municipalities. Mr. Billie, as he was affectionately known, did more than deliver the mail. He provided "personal service." Mr. Billie provided anything a person might need to purchase from the post office. All a customer needed to do was leave the flag up on their mailbox.

One elderly woman had trouble starting her lawn mower, so whenever she needed to use it, she would simply leave it by her mailbox, raise the flag, and when Mr. Billie came by, he would start it for her! Mr. Billie gave a new definition to the phrase "public servant."

True Christian servants rarely think of themselves as doing anything other than the ordinary, when what they actually do is quite extraordinary! The apostle Paul called himself a slave to Christ, yet he was too concerned about being a good servant to ever worry about being a real slave. Why? Because true servants are motivated by love. It is love they know they have received from Christ. And it is love they give.

One thing I do: Forgetting what is behind and straining toward what is ahead, I press on toward the goal.
Philippians 3:13-14 NIV

A critical spirit is like poison ivy—
it only takes a little contact to spread
its poison.

146

GLENN Van Ekeren tells about an experience he had with his son one summer vacation. For the first couple of days, his son Matt misbehaved constantly. Glenn seemed to be continually correcting him. Thinking, *No son of mine is going to act this way,* he made it clear to his son in no uncertain terms that he expected him to start behaving.

Matt tried very hard to live up to his father's standards. In fact, later in the week a day went by in which he hadn't done a single thing that called for correcting. That night, after Matt had said his prayers and jumped into bed, Glenn noticed that Matt's bottom lip began to quiver. "What's the matter, buddy?" he asked his son. Barely able to speak, Matt looked up at his father with tear-filled eyes and asked, "Daddy, haven't I been a good boy today?"

Glenn said, "Those words cut through my parental arrogance like a knife. I had been quick to criticize and correct his misbehavior but failed to mention my pleasure with his attempt to be a good boy. My son taught me never to put my children to bed without a word of appreciation and encouragement."

But avoid worldly and empty chatter, for it will lead to further ungodliness, and their talk will spread like gangrene.
2 Timothy 2:16-17 NASB

Laziness and poverty are cousins.

ONE day, a grandfather told his grandchildren about his coming to America. He told of the trains and ship that he took from his home in Eastern Europe. He told of being processed at Ellis Island and how he had gone to a cafeteria in lower Manhattan to get something to eat. There, he sat down at an empty table and waited quite some time for someone to take his order. Nobody came. Finally, a woman with a tray full of food sat down opposite him and explained to him how a cafeteria works.

She said, "You start at that end, and then go along the food line and pick out what you want. At the other end, they'll tell you how much you have to pay."

The grandfather reflected a moment and then said, "I soon learned that's how everything works in America. Life's a cafeteria here. You can get anything you want if you are willing to pay the price. But you'll never get what you want if you wait for someone to bring it to you."

The difference between where you are and where you want to be can often be summed up in one word: work.

Yet a little sleep, a little slumber, a little folding of the hands to sleep: So shall thy poverty come as one that travelleth; and thy want as an armed man.

Proverbs 24:33-34

Language is the expression of thought.
Every time you speak, your mind is
on parade.

A WOMAN was visiting her brother and his family one time when her nephew suddenly stopped in the midst of his play and steadily gazed up at her. "What are you thinking about?" she asked him. "Auntie, you're a Christian, aren't you?" he finally asked.

"I hope so, dear," she replied.

"But you never talk about Jesus." he said. "If you loved Him very much, wouldn't you talk about Him sometimes?"

The aunt, taken aback a bit, stammered a reply. "We may love a person without speaking of him," she said.

"Can we?" her nephew asked innocently. "I didn't know that. You talk about your papa and mamma and your brothers and sisters all the time. And you talk about other people too, even me, but not Jesus."

"Well, yes," the aunt admitted, her heart quickened with conviction. "I suppose that's been so."

"Let's talk about Jesus sometime," her nephew concluded before getting up to go outside to play. And then with a backward wink, he added, "Cause I love Him, too, and I like to talk about Him."

We talk about what and who matters the most to us. And what we say reveals how we feel about them.

The good man brings good things out of the good stored up in his heart. . . . For out of the overflow of his heart his mouth speaks.
Luke 6:45 NIV

The hardest secret for a man to keep is his opinion of himself.

A LITTLE Swiss watch had been made with the smallest of parts and the greatest of skill. It ran with tremendous precision, to the great delight of its owner. Still, the watch was dissatisfied with its restricted sphere of influence. It envied the high and lofty position of the great clock on the tower of City Hall.

One day as the little watch and its owner passed City Hall, the tiny watch exclaimed, "I sure wish I could be way up there! I could serve many people instead of just one." The watch's owner looked down and said, "I know someone who has a key to the tower. Little watch, you shall have your opportunity!"

The next day, a slender thread was let down from the tower and the little watch was tied to it. The watch was pulled up the side of the tower—higher and higher it rose! Of course, when it reached the top, it was completely lost to view. "Oh my," said the watch. "My elevation has resulted in my annihilation!"

If you desire to trade your current sphere of small influence for a larger one, be patient. The Lord will elevate you in His timing.

For I say, through the grace given unto me, to every man that is among you, not to think of himself more highly than he ought to think.

Romans 12:3

Even a woodpecker owes his success to the fact that he uses his head.

A WOMAN was sitting in her den one day when a small black snake suddenly appeared, slithered across the floor, and made its way under the couch. The woman promptly ran to the bathroom to get her husband, who was taking a shower. Running from the shower with only a towel around his waist, he grabbed a broom handle and began poking under the couch.

At this point, the family dog awoke. Curious, he came up behind the husband and touched his cold nose to the back of the man's heel. The man, surmising that the snake had bitten him on the heel, fainted dead away. The wife concluded that her husband had overexerted himself and collapsed with a heart attack. She ran from the house to a hospital just one block away. The ambulance drivers promptly returned with her to the house and placed the man on a stretcher. As they were carrying him out of the house, the snake reappeared from beneath the couch. One of the drivers became so excited that he dropped his end of the stretcher and consequently broke the husband's leg. Seeing her husband's twisted leg, the wife collapsed.

Meanwhile, the snake slithered quietly away!

But you, keep your head in all situations.

2 Timothy 4:5 NIV

You can accomplish more
in one hour with God than
one lifetime without Him.

RACHEL and Jim owned a commercial building, half of which Jim used for his dental practice. For fifteen years, they had no difficulty in renting out the other half. They counted on the extra income to pay their bills; then they lost their renter. A real estate agent told them, "Forget about advertising for awhile. Absolutely nobody is renting."

To ease her worries, Rachel started swimming laps at a local pool. One day when she was feeling especially anxious, she decided to pray as she swam, using the alphabet to keep track of her laps. She focused on adjectives to describe God, starting with the letter A. "You are the *almighty* God," she prayed on lap one. "A *benevolent* God, a *beautiful* God," she prayed on the next lap, and then, "You are a *caring, creative, can-do* God." By the time she had completed twenty-six laps, an hour had passed and her fears were gone. She *knew* God would provide.

A short time later, a physical therapist saw the "For Rent" sign, and she and her partner quickly rented the space. Rachel still prays while swimming laps. "After all," she says, "I've discovered God's goodness stretches from A to Z!"

With God all things are possible.

Matthew 19:26

When things go wrong, don't go wrong with them.

MEDICAL missionary Dr. Lambie, formerly of Abyssinia, forded many swift and bridgeless streams in Africa. The natives taught him the best way to complete a hazardous crossing.

The danger in crossing a stream lies in being swept off one's feet and carried downstream to deep water or being hurled to death against hidden rocks. A man can avoid this by finding a large stone—the heavier the better—lifting it to his shoulder, and carrying it across the stream, using the stone as a ballast. The extra weight of the stone keeps his feet solid on the stream bed.

In telling of this technique, Dr. Lambie drew an application to life: "While crossing the dangerous stream of life . . . we need the ballast of burden-bearing . . . to keep us from being swept off our feet."

This does not mean that we should seek out troubles or give in to our own problems. What it does mean is as we look around us, we help others shoulder their burdens and accept their help in bearing our own load. It's easy to become overwhelmed while carrying only your own burden. Shared burdens, however, travel lighter and provide the bearer stability.

Enter not into the path of the wicked,
and go not in the way of evil men.
❧ Proverbs 4:14 ❧

*T*wo things are hard on the heart—
running up stairs and running
down people.

A faculty member at a university had become very distraught over the weaknesses of a particular administrator. He allowed himself to think about the man constantly. Hateful thoughts so preoccupied him that it affected the quality of his relationships with his family, his friends, and his colleagues. He finally concluded that he should accept a teaching appointment elsewhere.

A friend asked him, "Wouldn't you really prefer to teach at this university, if the man were not here?"

"Of course," the man responded, "but as long as he is here, then my staying is too disruptive to everything in my life. I have to go."

The friend then asked, "Why have you made this administrator the center of your life?" As much as the man tried to deny the truth of this, he finally had to admit that he had allowed one individual and his weaknesses to distort his entire view of life. Still, it was not the administrator's doing. It was his own. From that day forward, he focused on his students and his teaching, and he found new joy in his "old job."

When you concentrate on running others down, the one who truly gets run down is you.

Let no corrupt communication proceed out of your mouth,
but that which is good to the use of edifying,
that it may minister grace unto the hearers.
Ephesians 4:29

*T*he best way to get even is to forget.

162

IN his book, *Beneath the Cross of Jesus*, A. Leonard Griffith tells the story of a young Korean exchange student, who left his apartment on the evening of April 25, 1958, to mail a letter to his parents. As he turned from the mailbox, he was met by eleven leather-jacketed teenage boys who beat him and left him lying dead in the gutter.

Philadelphia cried out for vengeance. The district attorney planned to seek the death penalty. Then, this letter arrived, signed by the boy's parents and twenty other relatives in Korea: "Our family has met together and we have decided to petition that the most generous treatment possible . . . be given to those who have committed this criminal action. . . . As evidence of our sincere hope contained in this petition, we have decided to save money to start a fund to be used for the religious, educational, vocational, and social guidance of the boys when they are released. . . . We have dared to express our hope with a spirit received from the gospel of our Savior Jesus Christ Who died for our sins."

When we forgive it takes us from victim to victor.

But love ye your enemies, and do good, and lend,
hoping for nothing again; and your reward shall be great.
Luke 6:35

Humor is to life what shock absorbers are to automobiles.

STANDUP comedian and author David Brenner was signing books in a San Francisco bookstore when a young man handed him a copy and said softly, "I want to thank you for saving my life." Brenner replied flippantly, "That's okay." The young man stood his ground and said, "No, I really mean it."

Brenner stopped and looked at him. The man said, "My father died. He was my best friend. I couldn't stop crying for weeks. I decided to take my own life. The night I was going to do it, I happened to have the TV on. You were hosting *The Tonight Show*. Next thing I knew I was watching you and laughing. Then I started laughing hysterically. I realized then that if I was able to laugh, I was able to live. So I want to thank you for saving my life." Humbled and grateful, Brenner shook his hand and said, "No, I thank you."

Laughter does more than help us escape our problems. It sometimes gives us the courage to face them. Author Barbara Johnson has said: "Laughter is like changing a baby's diaper. It doesn't permanently solve any problems, but it makes things more acceptable for awhile."

A merry heart doeth good like a medicine:
but a broken spirit drieth the bones.
🙟 Proverbs 17:22 🙝

$\mathcal{A}$ man wrapped up in himself
makes a very small package.

A pompous city man, turned farmer, was showing a young boy around his acreage. As they drove through field after field, the man bragged incessantly about his accomplishments and how he had started from scratch as a young man and worked his way up through the business world. He told how he had earned far more money than had been necessary to purchase the land and how he had invested thousands upon thousands of dollars to transform the formerly worthless farm into the agricultural paradise they were surveying. He told the boy of the amazing yield of his crops, and the lushness of the new spring planting.

Finally he pointed toward the stacked hay, the full granary, and the boxes of produce and declared, "And I grew it all by myself, sonny. Started with nothing, and now look at it!"

"From nothing?" echoed the duly impressed lad. "That's right," said the man. "From nothing."

"Wow," the young boy said, pausing to reflect for a few seconds. "My dad farms, but he needs seed to grow his crops."

When we get wrapped up in ourselves and our accomplishments, we often forget that we didn't get there alone—no one can.

A fool finds no pleasure in understanding
but delights in airing his own opinions.
Proverbs 18:2 NIV

*I*t takes more to plow a
field than merely turning it
over in your mind.

AN author once sought to escape city life by moving to a little house in the country. His house was located across the street from a farm; and from his library window, he often looked up from his writing to watch as his neighbor engaged in a wide variety of jobs that needed to be done on his farm.

He watched as the man mended the fence after his cattle had broken through it. He watched as the man replanted a field after a heavy deluge washed out a new planting. He watched as he made repairs to his tractor and removed several large stones from his field after a tractor blade broke. The farmer seemed to work from sunup to sundown, doing battle against the elements and facing one problem after another. The author began to wonder about the man's optimism.

One day the author strolled from his cottage to talk to the farmer. "You amaze me," he said after he greeted his neighbor. "You never seem to lose heart. Do you always hope for the best?"

The farmer thought for a moment and with eyes flashing he replied, "No, I don't hope for it; I hop for it!"

Work with your hands, just as we commanded you;
so that you may behave properly toward
outsiders and not be in any need.
1 Thessalonians 4:11-12 NASB

The heart of a man cannot
be determined by the size of
his pocketbook.

AFTER winning a tournament, golfer Robert De Vincenzo received his check on the eighteenth green, flashed a smile for the cameras, and then walked to the clubhouse alone. As he went to his car, he was approached by a sad-eyed young woman who said to him, "It's a good day for you, but I have a baby with an incurable blood disease. The doctors say she will die." De Vincenzo paused and then asked, "May I help your little girl?" He then took out a pen, endorsed his prize check, and then pressed it into her hand. "Make some good days for the baby," he said.

A week later as he was having lunch at a country club, a PGA official approached him, saying, "Some of the boys told me you met a young woman in the parking lot after you won the tournament." De Vincenzo nodded. The official said, "Well, she's a phony. She has no sick baby. She fleeced you, my friend."

The golfer looked up and asked, "You mean that there is no dying baby?" The official nodded. De Vincenzo grinned and said, "That's the best news I've heard all week."

A giver has a generous heart.

For what shall it profit a man, if he shall gain the whole world, and lose his own soul? Or what shall a man give in exchange for his soul?

Mark 8:36-37

You can easily determine the caliber of a person by the amount of opposition it takes to discourage him.

A biology student found a cocoon one day and brought it to his teacher. She put it in a glass box with a warming lamp. About a week later, the students saw a small opening appear on the cocoon. Suddenly, tiny antennae appeared. The students watched the progress of the emerging insect throughout the day. By noon it had freed its listless wings. It wiggled and shook, but try as it might, it could not seem to force its body through the small opening. One student decided to snip off the end of the cocoon to help the insect. Out it plopped. Only the top half of it looked like a butterfly, however. The bottom half was large and swollen. The insect crawled about, dragging its listless wings; and a short time later, it died.

The next day, the biology teacher explained that the butterfly's struggle to get through the tiny opening is necessary in order to force fluids from the swollen body into the wings so they will be strong enough to fly. Without the struggle, the wings never develop.

Rather than working to avoid struggle in life, we should work through our struggles. Our struggles develop inner character.

If thou faint in the day of adversity, thy strength is small.
Proverbs 24:10

People know what you are by what they see, not by what they hear.

WHILE doing research for a doctoral thesis, a young man spent a year with a group of Navajo Indians on a reservation in the Southwest. He lived with one family, sleeping in their hut, eating their food, working with them, and generally living their life.

The grandmother of the family spoke no English, yet a very close friendship formed between the grandmother and the student. They seemed to share the common language of love, and they intuitively understood each other. Over the months they each learned bits and pieces of the other's language.

When it was time for the young man to return to the university and write his thesis, the tribe held a going-away celebration for him. It was marked by sadness since he had developed a close relationship with all the villagers. As he prepared to get into his pickup truck and drive away, the old grandmother came to tell him good-bye. With tears streaming from her eyes, she placed her hands on either side of his face, looked directly into his eyes, and said, "I like me best when I'm with you."

True friendship is letting those around you not only be themselves, but be their best.

Let your light so shine before men,
that they may see your good works,
and glorify your Father which is in heaven.
❧ Matthew 5:16 ☙

*Q*uite often when a man thinks
his mind is getting broader,
it's only his conscience stretching.

ONE day, a mother was helping her son with his spelling assignment, and they came to the words *conscious* and *conscience*. She asked her son, "Do you know the difference between these two words?"

He immediately replied, "Sure, Mom. 'Conscious' is when you are aware of something. And, 'conscience' is when you wish you weren't."

The conscience is like a sharp square peg in our hearts. When we are confronted by a situation that calls for a decision on what is wrong or right, that square peg begins to turn. Its corners cut into our hearts, warning us that we are facing a situation in which we must make a choice against evil and for good.

If the conscience is ignored time after time, however, the corners of the square peg are gradually worn down, and it becomes a circle that twists and turns at will. Our heart becomes callused and unfeeling. When that circle turns within our hearts, it produces no inner warning. In effect, we are left without a conscience.

A sound conscience is truly a gift from God. As we obey Him and listen to our conscience, our hearts become even more sensitive to what is right.

> *Unto the pure all things are pure: but unto them*
> *that are defiled and unbelieving is nothing pure;*
> *but even their mind and conscience is defiled.*
> Titus 1:15

We make a living by what we get— we make a life by what we give.

TWO brothers farmed together. They lived in separate houses but met each morning to work together in the fields. One brother married and had a large family. The other lived alone. Still, they divided the harvest equally.

One night the single brother thought, *My brother is struggling to support a large family, but I get half of the harvest.* With love in his heart, he gathered a box of things he had purchased from his earnings. He planned to slip over to his brother's shed, unload the basket, and never say a word about it.

That same night, the married brother thought, *My brother is alone. He doesn't know the joys of a family.* Out of love, he decided to take over a basket with a quilt, homemade bread, and preserves to warm his brother's home. He planned to leave the items on his porch and never say a word.

As the brothers stealthily made their way to each other's home, they bumped into one other. They were forced to admit what they were doing and there in the darkness, they cried and embraced, each man realizing that his greatest wealth was a brother who respected and loved him.

Remember the words of the Lord Jesus, how he said,
It is more blessed to give than to receive.

Acts 20:35

179

*O*ur days are identical suitcases—
all the same size—but some people
can pack more into them than others.

SPARKY didn't have much going for him. He failed every subject in the eighth grade, and in high school, he flunked Latin, algebra, English, and physics. He made the golf team, but promptly lost the only important match of the season, and then lost the consolation match. He was awkward socially; he never once asked a girl to go out on a date.

One thing was important to Sparky, however—drawing. He was proud of his artwork, even though no one else appreciated it. He submitted cartoons to the editors of his high school yearbook, but they were turned down. Even so, Sparky aspired to be an artist. After high school, he sent samples of his artwork to Walt Disney Studios. Again, he was turned down.

Still, Sparky didn't quit packing his suitcase! He decided to write his autobiography in cartoons. The character he created became famous worldwide—the subject not only of cartoon strips but countless books, television shows, and licensing opportunities. Sparky, you see, was Charles Schulz, creator of the "Peanuts" comic strip. Like his character, Charlie Brown, Schulz may not have been able to do many things. But, he made the most of what he could do!

Be very careful, then, how you live—not as unwise but as wise,
making the most of every opportunity.
Ephesians 5:15-16 NIV

Living would be easier if men showed as much patience at home as they do when they're fishing.

FIRMIN Abautiz was known as a man of serene disposition. Nobody in his town could recall his having lost his temper at any time during his eighty-seven years. One man, who doubted the possibility that a person could be so unflappable, made a deal with a housekeeper, offering her money if she could provoke him to anger.

The housekeeper knew that Abautiz was very fond of a comfortable, orderly bed, so she neglected to make his bed one day. The next morning, Abautiz kindly reminded her of the undone chore. The next night, Abautiz again found an unmade bed; and the following morning, he again called it to her attention. She made a lame excuse, which he kindly accepted.

On the third morning, Abautiz said, "You still have not made my bed; it is evident you are determined not to do it. Well, I suppose you find the job troublesome; but it is of little consequence, for I begin to be used to it already." Moved by such goodness, the woman called off the deal and never again failed to make his bed as comfortable as possible!

Patience and kindness get results far better than anger and wrath could produce.

You husbands likewise, live with
your wives in an understanding way.
1 Peter 3:7 NASB

*S*ome people succeed because they
are destined to, but most people succeed
because they are determined to.

THERE once was a Louisville University quarterback who dreamed of playing pro football. Upon graduation, however, no pro team drafted him. So, he wrote to several teams and finally got an opportunity to try out for the Pittsburgh Steelers. He gave his best effort but wasn't chosen. His friends said, "You got a raw deal. I guess it's time to hang up your cleats." But the young athlete didn't give up.

He continued to knock on doors and write letters. Finally, he received another invitation. But again, he didn't make the team.

Most people would have given up long before this point, but not Johnny. He was fanatic about his dream. From his early days of playing sandlot football, he had been obsessed with this goal. So, patiently and persistently, he continued to pursue try-out opportunities. Finally, he was invited to try out for the Baltimore team, and he made the third string! Through training and many long hours of drills and fitness building, he worked his way up to be starting quarterback. Indeed, he became one of the greatest quarterbacks ever to play in the NFL. The dreamer's name? Johnny Unitas.

Keep driving until you arrive at your goal line!

Stand your ground, and after you
have done everything. . . . Stand firm then.
Ephesians 6:13-14 NIV

$\mathcal{G}$od intervenes in the affairs
of men by invitation only.

THERE once was a saintly man who lived on the edge of poverty, by his own choice. He distributed the money he earned equally between himself and the poor. The man's adult son was among those who had difficulty making ends meet, so the man gave him just enough to keep body and soul together, even as he continued to help others who found themselves in dire need. One day the father was asked why he paid so little attention to his son's personal needs while the bulk of his attention went to others. "You could help your son much more," his critic said, "if you would help strangers less."

"Ah," the man replied wisely, "but if I were to meet all my son's requirements, would he perhaps forget the necessity of relying upon the Lord? If that became the case, I would not be helping my son at all!"

God forbid that we find ourselves feeling totally self-sufficient. It is in that dark corner that pride lurks. Once pride takes over, we see little reason to invite the Lord to do His work in our lives. Take inventory. Have you invited God into the affairs of your life lately?

Behold, I stand at the door, and knock: if any man hear
my voice, and open the door, I will come in to him,
and will sup with him, and he with me.
Revelation 3:20

The difference between ordinary
and extraordinary is that little extra.

CHARLES F. Kettering, a noted scientist and inventor, believed that the easiest way to overcome defeat was simply to completely ignore the possibility of failure and keep forging ahead. He once gave an address to Denison University on this theme. He told how he had once given a tough project assignment to a young research worker in a laboratory at General Motors. He wanted to see how the man would react to a difficult problem, so he kept from him notes about the project that had been filed in the lab's library. These notes, written by expert researchers, included various sets of statistics and formulas that proved the assignment the young man had been given was impossible.

The young research worker set his mind to the project and worked virtually night and day for weeks. He refused to give up or think the project impossible. One day he came confidently to Kettering to show him his work. He had succeeded in doing the impossible!

A little extra time, a little extra effort, a little extra care, a little extra attention sometimes makes all the difference between success and failure, and not only that, but the difference between good and great.

Whatsoever thy hand findeth to do, do it with thy might;
for there is no work, nor device, nor knowledge,
nor wisdom, in the grave, whither thou goest.
Ecclesiastes 9:10

$\mathscr{S}$wallowing angry words is much better than having to eat them.

A SMALL-town newspaper developed a column specifically to interview couples who had reached their golden wedding anniversary. A brief history of the couple celebrating fifty years of marriage was outlined. Then, the newspaper posed the same question to each spouse: "To what do you attribute the success of your marriage?" Many of the couples approaching this milestone knew they were going to be interviewed and they gave long thought to the wisest and most practical advice they could give. Some advocated total honesty, others a shared faith, and others abundant communication.

One man lovingly glanced at his wife and then replied: "The secret of our fifty years of marital harmony is quite simple. My wife and I made an agreement the day we were married. If she was bothered or upset about something, she was to get it off her chest and out in the open. And, if I was mad at her about something, we agreed I would take a walk. So, I guess you can attribute our marital success to the fact that I have led largely an outdoor life."

In finding a way to release anger and frustration, make sure your loved ones don't become your targets.

A fool uttereth all his mind: but a wise man
keepeth it in till afterwards.
Proverbs 29:11

he company you keep will
determine the trouble you meet.

HAVE you ever seen an empty oyster shell? You may have wondered, *How did the oyster get out?* You might look for a very small hole in the top of the shell. Such a hole is made by a whelk. This little ocean creature has an appendage that works somewhat like an auger. With it, the whelk bores into the oyster shell and then sucks the oyster through the hole, little by little, until it has devoured it all. Though small, a whelk can do great harm!

Very often, we allow another person's angry outbursts to bore a hole into our good nature and rob us of our otherwise sunny disposition. If we aren't careful, we can become irritated to the point where genuine anger and bitterness begin to seethe in us. When that happens, we are in very real danger of experiencing disease, disharmony, and discord.

One of the best things you can do is to simply avoid those people whom you find irksome, continually critical, or habitually angry at life, as well as those who seem to delight in needling you. In other words, stay out of the way of whelks. You'll be healthier and happier for it!

Make no friendship with an angry man;
and with a furious man thou shalt not go:
Lest thou learn his ways, and get a snare to thy soul.
Proverbs 22:24-25

*T*oo many parents are not on spanking terms with their children.

A BOY once made headlines as the result of his repeated vandalism. Even though he came from a well-to-do family, he was a perfect example of a juvenile delinquent. A reporter quizzed the boy in detention, asking, "Why do you feel the need to destroy property? Are you angry?" The boy just shrugged his shoulders and turned away. The reporter persisted, "Weren't you afraid of getting a licking from your parents?"

At this the boy looked at the reporter, and said, "I've never had a licking in my life." The tone of his voice, however, was not one of bitterness, but of sadness. The reporter talked with him further and realized that this young boy felt that his parents didn't care one whit about him. The young man concluded the interview by declaring that if the police turned him loose, he would continue to take out his vengeance on the neighborhood until one or the other of his folks cared enough to stop him.

Spanking is not abuse. Abuse is rooted in a parent's uncontrolled expression of power. Spanking is discipline intended to restrain and rechannel a child's uncontrolled expression of power! Abuse never has a place. Spanking sometimes does.

He who spares his rod hates his son,
But he who loves him disciplines him diligently.
Proverbs 13:24 NASB

195

*M*an cannot discover new oceans
unless he has the courage to
lose sight of the shore.

CENTURIES ago, when a mapmaker would run out of known world before he ran out of parchment, he often would sketch a dragon at the edge of the scroll. This was intended to be a sign to the explorer that he was entering unknown territory at his own risk.

Many explorers, however, did not perceive the dragon as a mapmaker's warning sign, but rather, as a prophecy. They foresaw disaster and doom beyond the known worlds they traversed. Their fear kept them from pushing on to discover new lands and peoples.

Other more adventuresome travelers saw the dragon as a sign of opportunity, the doorway to a new territory worth exploring.

Each of us has a mental map that contains the information we use for guidance as we explore each new day. Like the maps of long ago, our mental maps have edges, and sometimes those edges seem to be marked by dragons—fears. At times, our fears may be valid. But at other times, our fears may keep us from discovering more of this world or more about other people, including ourselves. Don't let fear keep you from all that God desires for you to explore and to know!

And when Peter was come down out of the ship,
he walked on the water, to go to Jesus.
Matthew 14:29

197

*T*he heart is the happiest
when it beats for others.

ONE of the people most admired by Charles Swindoll is Dawson Trotman, who died after rescuing two drowning girls. Says Swindoll:

> When Dawson Trotman passed away he probably left a legacy of discipleship on this earth that will never be matched except perhaps in the life of Jesus Christ Himself. I've become a real student of Dawson Trotman and believe wholeheartedly in the methods of discipleship that he taught and emulated throughout his days. . . . He died of all things in the midst of an area that he was expert in—he drowned. He was an expert swimmer. The last few moments he had in the water he lifted one girl out. He went down and got the other girl and lifted her out, and then submerged and was not found again until the dragnet found him a few hours later. . . . *Time* ran an article on Trotman's life, and they put a caption beneath his name. It read, "Always Holding Somebody Up." In one sentence, that was Trotman's life investment in people . . . holding them up.

Discipleship is not having others follow you, as much as it is lifting others up to see the Lord.

Greater love hath no man than this,
that a man lay down his life for his friends.
John 15:13

One thing you can learn by watching the clock is that it passes time by keeping its hands busy.

A MAN was once drawn by the idea that living in "quiet contemplation away from human society" was the sure path to happiness. He wandered into the desert to become a hermit. He found a cave near a spring where he could obtain water and grow a few plants for food. Feeling self-sufficient, he spent many idle hours in solitude. Eventually, the hours of the day dragged by. Feeling more wretched than holy, he cried, "Father God, let me die. I am weary of this life." Exhausted, he fell asleep and dreamed that an angel stood before him, saying, "Cut down the palm tree that grows near the spring and turn its fibers into a rope."

The hermit awoke and with great effort and many hours of toil, he felled the palm and made a coil of rope from it. Again the angel appeared to him, saying, "I can tell you are no longer weary of life. Go back into the world with your rope and find employment with it. Let it remind you toil is sweet."

Work not only benefits the mind and wallet, but the body and soul. Work keeps all parts of the human machine in order.

He also that is slothful in his work is brother
to him that is a great waster.
Proverbs 18:9

*N*ow there's even a "dial-a-prayer"
for atheists. You call a number
and nobody answers.

THE story is told of a colony of mice who made their home in the bottom of a large upright piano. To them, music was frequent, even routine. It filled all the dark spaces with lovely melodies and harmonies.

At first, the mice were impressed by the music. They drew comfort and wonder from the thought that "Someone" made the music—though invisible to them, yet close to them. They loved to tell stories about the "Great Unseen Player."

Then one day an adventurous mouse climbed up part of the way in the piano and returned with an elaborate explanation about how the music was made. Wires were the secret—tightly stretched wires of various lengths that vibrated and trembled from time to time. A second mouse ventured forth and came back telling of hammers, many hammers dancing and leaping on the wires. The mice decided they must revise their old opinions and stories. The theory they developed was complicated, but complete with evidence. In the end, the mice concluded that they lived in a purely mechanical and mathematical world. The story of the "Great Unseen Player" was relegated to mere myth.

But the "Unseen Player" continued to play nonetheless.

The fool hath said in his heart, There is no God.
Psalm 14:1

$\mathcal{T}$he best inheritance
a father can leave
his children is a good
example.

A YOUNG woman relates that when she was a little girl, her father, an artist, would often be busy at his easel, mixing oils and painting on his big canvases while she sat nearby on the floor, working just as hard with her crayons and a coloring book.

Many a time, he would set his brushes aside and lift her up onto his lap. Then he'd curl her little hand around one of his brushes, enfolding it with his own larger and stronger hand. And ever so gently, he would guide her hand, dipping it into the palette and mixing the burnt umbers and raw siennas, and then stroke the wet, shiny paint onto the canvas before them both. The little girl watched in amazement as, together, they made something beautiful. Little did this father know that he was giving his daughter skills that would bring great fulfillment to her life.

Today Joni Tada, a quadriplegic since a diving accident during her teen years, is still painting, but with a paintbrush in her mouth. Much of her earnings is channeled into ministry to help others. Her compassion, too, is a reflection of that shown her by a loving, tender father.

As ye know how we exhorted and comforted and charged every one of you, as a father doth his children.
1 Thessalonians 2:11

Additional copies of this book are available
from your local bookstore.

Also look for these titles from Honor Books.

God's Little Devotional Book for Women, Special Gift Edition
God's Little Devotional Bible
God's Little Devotional Book on Success
God's Little Devotional Book for Men
God's Little Book of Promises

Honor Books
Tulsa, Oklahoma